A[illegible] [illegible]er

STRATEGIC PROPERTY INVESTING

What works and what doesn't in a complex UK residential property market

Published by Known Publishing, 2021

ISBN: 978-1-913036-22-5

KNOWN

www.get-known.co.uk

Contents

PART 2 /67

INVESTING

Foreword

In producing this timely book, Anna starts out in exactly the right way:

"For more than 20 years, UK residential property has been seen as one of the best investments available. The trouble is the market has changed. Approaches that worked before are now less profitable, if profitable at all."

Property investment isn't easy. If it was once straightforward, it is much harder now. One of the most common investment myths is that it is easy to make money consistently from property, and that you do not need professional help.

One of our mutual one-time colleagues at Cambridge argued that residential property investment was 'a hedge against under-employment'. What he meant was that if we owned residential property investments and decided to retire, or lost our jobs, or became less fully employed, we could use our now-free time to work on the properties and be the property manager, saving fees.

My own experience is a confusion of emotion and finance, and a lack of clarity regarding my strategic objectives. Might I live in the property one day? Do I like the area and the neighbours? Maybe to me, residential property investment was a hedge against eviction.

Whichever professor's hedge you prefer or object to the most, you would be wise to read Anna's book.

We learn that the most common, expensive mistakes result from the lack of a clear strategy that is suited to the investor, their goals, situation and the market; the right deal criteria, a well-managed deal pipeline and quality transactions; and strong professional asset management. The concise and clear advice contained within will help you to avoid the mistakes that many of us – including Professors of Real Estate Investment – make in the residential property investment market.

Andrew Baum
University of Oxford

JANUARY 2020

PART I

Context: Understanding The UK Residential Property Market

Introduction

WHY NOW?

UK residential property is seen by many as one of the best investments available. However, the market has changed. As a result, approaches that worked before aren't working anymore.

Margins are being squeezed. Even well-funded, highly intelligent investors like those I've worked with over the years are facing the prospect of low, no or even negative real returns. Yet, in this uncertain, fast-changing low interest rate environment, it has never been more important to invest. Across the board, investors are seeking a way to grow their wealth and generate income that will be safe, secure and stable now and for years to come.

The unfortunate truth is that as market and regulatory pressures have risen, so have the chances of making poor decisions and expensive mistakes. Many investors fear wasting time, money and effort. Without a clear understanding of what is happening in the market and an approach that works throughout market changes, they may be right.

To succeed, investors must understand and navigate a complicated environment, they must know what works and what doesn't, and they must be more strategic in their approach.

WHO IS THIS BOOK FOR?

This book is written primarily for the kind of investor I have worked with throughout my career. Typically, they already have funds ready to invest and they already know they want to invest in UK residential property as a way to diversify, grow wealth and earn additional income. Increasingly, they also know that they need a new approach to investing in this complex market, in order to make the right decisions and minimise the risk of future regrets from missing out or losing time and money.

If this sounds like you, read on.

WHO AM I?

You might be wondering who I am, and why I've written this book.

I'm Anna, a property investor, strategist, podcast host and, now, the author of this book.

I Co-Founded SPI Capital, a real estate consultancy with a social conscience supporting investors who want to make the most of the opportunities in the current market financially, whilst delivering social value.

Before this, I developed the strategy and built the seed portfolio for a HNWI-backed fund targeting a £100m+ housing portfolio, was involved with c. £2bn+ transactions as a Strategist at Deloitte and studied real estate at Cambridge.

Along the way, I've had the privilege of being recognised as one of Management Today's '35 Women Under 35' and Bisnow's 'Women Leading Real Estate', and giving a TedX talk on property investment.

I host The Return: Property & Investment Podcast (bit.ly/returnpodcast), which has become a leading podcast in the sector.

I also comment in and write regularly for publications including the BBC, Financial Times and Forbes on property market trends and investing.

So, with all this going on, why did I give up my weekends for so many months to write this book in the first place? The property industry is hardly short of content.

The short story is, my work and research highlighted a gap in the market for a clear, reliable guide to what's really happening in the UK residential property market, and how investors with funding can navigate through market changes both profitably and sustainably.

In many ways, there has never been a better time to invest in the UK residential market. Investor appetite and tenant demand are growing. What I believe needs to change is the way investors approach it.

I've come to believe that the most significant determinant of success for property investors is having the right strategy. Perhaps the biggest mistake an investor can make is not understanding the market and not having a clear strategy, before they invest.

This book aims to empower investors like you to navigate the complexity and develop a strategy that you can be confident in, even in a fast-changing, uncertain context.

HOW IT WORKS

The first part of this book addresses how the market has changed.

The second part covers what to do about those changes, including what works and what doesn't, in a complex property market.

To explain what works, it includes a simple methodology, the 5As, which you can use to ensure you are taking the right approach. This is designed to enable you to make better decisions and minimise the risk of having future regrets from missing out or losing time and money in any market. Through each step in the methodology, the linchpin is strategy. Strategy both defines and is defined by the 5As. It is also what connects you today with where you want to be.

Each stage of the methodology includes frameworks, tools and take-away tips to enable you to quickly adopt a strategic approach suited to this complicated environment.

To illustrate what doesn't work, real-life examples highlight common, expensive mistakes throughout the book, so that you can avoid them.

Of course, I'd encourage you to read the whole book. However, we live in an age of 'busy-ness'. The average to-do list is already far too long. With this in mind, I've written it in a way that you won't have to read it from cover to cover to get value from the book.

If you don't have the time or inclination to read it all, skim through the contents and focus on the chapters that you feel will be most beneficial, as well as the *Strategy Soundbite: Chapter Summaries* and *Takeaway Tips.* These highlight the most important things you need to know about what works and what doesn't, in a complex UK residential property market.

CHAPTER 1

UK residential property investing: what it is, what it isn't and the problems investors are facing

The idea of UK residential property investment is more than a national obsession. For investors from across the world, it has come to be seen as one of the best investments available. This is for good reason. It offers compelling, stable returns in a way that is relatively easy to understand and implement.

This chapter will explain what I really mean by property investing and what the investors I work with really want. It will highlight the three biggest problems investors are facing and debunk some common misconceptions.

WHAT IS PROPERTY INVESTMENT?

The idea of property investment might seem simple. It's worth defining, as there are some common misunderstandings.

Investing is:

> *"...putting (money) into financial schemes, shares, property, or a commercial venture with the expectation of achieving a profit."*[1]

Investing in property is simply putting money into real estate assets, with the goal of taking more money out in the future. This can be through the direct purchase, ownership, management, rental and/or sale of land and buildings. It can also be indirect. For example, it might be via land banking schemes, property company shares, real estate investment trusts (REITs), or other investment trusts.[2]

Let's clarify a few things.

Firstly, property investing is not the same as property ownership. For many 'baby boomers', owning property has become both a signifier and determinant of success. It is central to the notion of stability and a comfortable life. Contrary to popular opinion, however, homeownership is not property investment. Robert Kiyosaki's bestselling book, *Rich Dad, Poor Dad*, popularised the idea that assets create income and liabilities create expenses.[3] In this school of thought, you take on a liability rather than an asset when you buy your own home.

Unless you're renting it out it will cost you money to hold it, and you can't guarantee it will go up in value.

The same goes for many hybrid opportunities. For example, let's say you buy a holiday home because you like it and hope to make some money as well, rather than select an investment with a pure profit motive. There's often a trade-off between how attractive properties are for you as a consumer as opposed to how they perform for you as an investor.

Secondly, for many investors, property is not just about making a profit, unlike other forms of investing. Property feels less risky, easier to understand, and more accessible than many other forms of investment. It is not just about the financials. The unique combination of tangibility, trust and time-tested strong performance means that, for many people, bricks and mortar feels like the safest place to store their wealth. It is more intuitive and, in the case of direct investments, easier to control than, say, ordinary or preference shares, investment trusts and exchange-traded funds.

The specialist knowledge that is required to invest successfully in the stock market can take years of training and qualifications to master. Even those who have mastered it can fail to understand the bigger picture, as illustrated by our most recent Global Financial Crisis.

An individual investor is often unable to control or fully understand such mainstream assets, due to the divorce between ownership and control. Meanwhile, there is an emotional pull towards property investment, lower barriers to entry and often the ability to touch, use and improve the asset. Its popularity has been echoed and exaggerated by the mainstream media. TV shows like *Homes Under*

The Hammer, Changing Rooms, Grand Designs, and articles in major news publications have made ordinary people feel like they can, and should, get involved with property investing.

WHAT PROPERTY INVESTING IS REALLY ABOUT

The truth is, for many of the investors I've worked with, property investing is not really about property or investing. Instead, it's about safety, security and stability. It's a way to solve the problem of financial dependence on a business or inheritance and build a legacy for the future. The added sweetener is it feels 'closer to home'.

As a result, when I talk about residential property investing, what I'm really talking about is a way to grow wealth, generate income and build a legacy without too much hassle in a way that seems simple. Over the last 20 years, UK buy-to-let rental properties have come to be seen as the ideal way for individual investors with limited time to make easy, safe, long-term profits.

THE PROBLEMS FACING UK RESIDENTIAL PROPERTY INVESTORS

Market and regulatory changes and uncertainties have profoundly affected the UK residential property market in recent years. I'll discuss these in more detail later in the book.

First, I'll explain the significance of these changes. The short story is this: approaches that worked previously won't anymore, particularly for the kinds of private investors that have come to dominate the private rental sector (hereon, PRS – of which 94% were individuals in 2018).[4] So traditional approaches provide lower and less certain returns. Profitable opportunities are harder to access. This comes at a time when financial security and confidence for the future command a premium.

These investors are facing three major problems in this complex environment.

PROBLEM 1: UNREWARDED

In this long-term low interest rate environment, there is a huge demand for stronger returns. Investors know that their capital is underperforming when it sits unused in a current account. Many investors feel unrewarded from their savings accounts, stocks picked via Self-Invested Personal Pensions (SIPPs), or even funds managed professionally. Yet approaches to property investing that once worked have become more costly and complicated thanks to the changes described later in this book. Further, approaches relying on capital growth for returns seem less likely to deliver, as interest rates cannot go much lower to encourage investors, and affordability constraints based on incomes restrict potential buyers.

Traditionally easy options in the property market are delivering lower returns, for example:

- Holding rental properties in personal names.
- Buying a property in an area with historically strong capital growth, such as London.
- Buying prime new build rental flats, off-plan or completed.

Newer, more flexible options, such as crowd-funded deals, offer great potential returns. However, they are in beta-testing mode. Performance remains unproven and inconsistent.

So property investors are earning less than before. More effort and risk are required to achieve a given return. This might be due to market dynamics or not investing in the right ways. It might be due to making snap decisions, making no decisions at all (delaying and letting time and opportunities slip by is still a decision), or implementing decisions unprofessionally.

PROBLEM 2: UNABLE TO ACCESS SUITABLE OPPORTUNITIES

In this more complex market, even the most intelligent, well-funded investors are struggling to access compelling property investment opportunities.

A lack of time, teams and knowledge can lead investors to dive into opportunities that seem, at face value, to be promising. Now though, the soft landing provided by a booming market can't be relied on. New regulations, along with a wider political will in favour of professional investors who are easier to regulate, mean additional checks, balances, standards and regulations. These must be managed carefully by investors and add to the challenges of investing.

Market, regulatory and tax changes mean that yield has become more important. The mantra of capital growth can no longer be assumed. Investments in London and the South East are performing less well.

Currently, 70% of UK residential property investors focus on properties within ten miles of where they live.[5] For investors located in these more expensive markets, investing further from home is more relevant, and geographical constraints become a bigger problem.

Geography, time, and new regulations to make the sector more professional are making a challenging prospect even harder. Specialised knowledge, experience, relevant contacts, time and attention are required.

PROBLEM 3: UNCERTAINTY

Property has historically been seen as one of the safest places for investors to store wealth, whilst earning returns. The security and confidence of having a stable portfolio that generates income and holds value throughout cycles are especially attractive in an uncertain environment. The appetite for income-producing investments that enable investors to grow wealth safely is strong. A low interest rate environment and an ageing population exaggerate this trend. Many face a shrinking pension pot, and a longer wait until they can access it. On a practical level, investors have looked to property to enhance a pension pot, create a back-up plan, or build a legacy to pass on to their children.

However, thanks to the fast pace of change in recent years, investor confidence is low. It's not just small- and medium-sized (SME) investors[6] who are struggling to make sense of a new reality. We all face an uncertain future. Investors of all scales lack clarity about how best to invest and where to focus at a time when the security and confidence that comes with a stable, profitable, income-generating portfolio is more desirable than ever.

PROPERTY CAN DELIVER WHAT INVESTORS WANT

Whatever their level of wealth, investors want to be rewarded. They want to feel confident about the future, regardless of what happens in the economy or their industry. They want this to be easy to understand and implement without it taking up their time. The good news is that, if it's done right, property still has the potential to deliver what investors want: easy access to ongoing profits and a more secure, confident future.

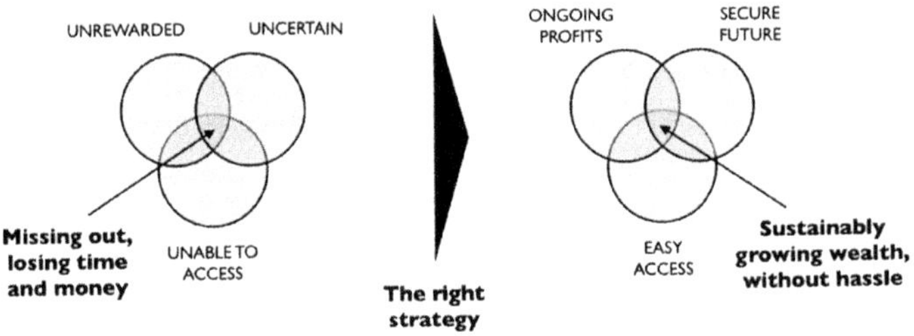

Figure 1.1 The right strategy can help investors to grow wealth, and avoid missing out.

In Figure 1.1, you can see that many investors fear missing out by losing time and money. They feel unrewarded by traditional approaches to investing in property and beyond, unable to access suitable, compelling opportunities, and uncertain about the future.

They need the right strategy to preserve and grow wealth without hassle. They want to achieve ongoing returns from investments that they feel confident in, regardless of what is happening in the market, without sacrificing their time and energy.

If you are like the investors I typically work with, you most likely want the same things.

STRATEGY SOUNDBITE CHAPTER SUMMARY

UK residential property continues to attract national and international attention. It is distinct from property ownership. It is distinct from other forms of investing. For many investors, property still feels like the best approach to achieving the outcomes they want.

Over the last twenty years, in particular, property has offered compelling, ongoing returns, confidence and certainty in a way that is clear, easy to understand and easy to implement. It has offered a solution for those who want to grow wealth without the hassle.

However, the current environment is leaving investors feeling unrewarded, unable to access suitable opportunities and uncertain about the future. Many previously profitable approaches are no longer working. The risks of losing time and money are compounded by the market context. This comes at a time when investors crave a secure financial future more than ever.

Increasingly, investors are achieving no returns or even negative real returns on equity, whether they have recognised this yet or not.

CHAPTER 2

Key concepts and what investors really want

Rather than getting technical and focusing on complex financial ratios to assess performance, this chapter will focus on what the investors I've worked with really care about in the context of UK residential property investment:

- How much money you are going to make: 'the absolute returns.'
- The chances of losing money: the risk associated with returns or 'risk/reward' ratio.
- How hard it will be: the effort you have to put in and 'effort/reward' ratio.
- What you are missing out on: the 'opportunity cost'.

These metrics can be used to make better investment decisions. They touch on both the art and science of investing.

HOW MUCH MONEY YOU ARE GOING TO MAKE: THE ABSOLUTE RETURNS

Definition: *Absolute returns are the profits achieved, expressed in total or annually.*

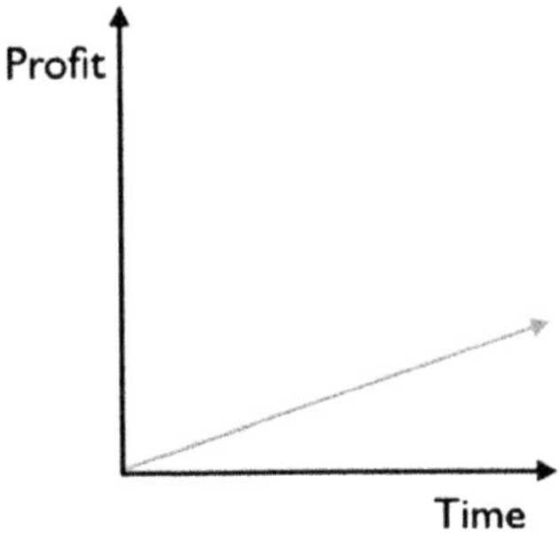

Figure 2.1: Absolute returns are the profits achieved over time.

Example: Calculated in simple terms, if you earn a 4% return each year, that's a 20% return over five years.

On an investment of £1,000,000, this would be £40,000 per year, and £200,000 over five years.

Using compound interest – what Einstein described as the 8th wonder of the world[7] you would earn £220,997 over the same period (compounding monthly).

Explanation: Absolute returns are generally provided on investment marketing materials. However, for many investors, this is the least helpful measure discussed in this chapter. Absolute profits ignore the realities of risk, effort and alternatives available. Still, absolute returns in property have been strong, thanks to the combination of capital growth and rental income.

UK property prices have risen since records began in 1952.[8] Despite volatility during recessions, UK property prices doubled every 9-10 years during this period. Combined with rental income and the ability to add value through refurbishments, buy-to-let landlords achieved returns of almost 1,400% between 1996 and 2014.[9]

I will go into more detail about market dynamics later in this book. The upshot is that the fundamentals of the UK housing market involve growing demand and constrained supply. This supply gap and upward pricing pressure on values and rents look likely to continue, meaning continued strong returns to residential property assets, other things being equal.

THE CHANCES OF LOSING MONEY: THE RISK ASSOCIATED WITH RETURNS OR RISK/REWARD RATIO

Definition: *Risk represents the chance of something going wrong and the uncertainty associated with returns. The risk/reward ratio is the level of returns, relative to risk.*

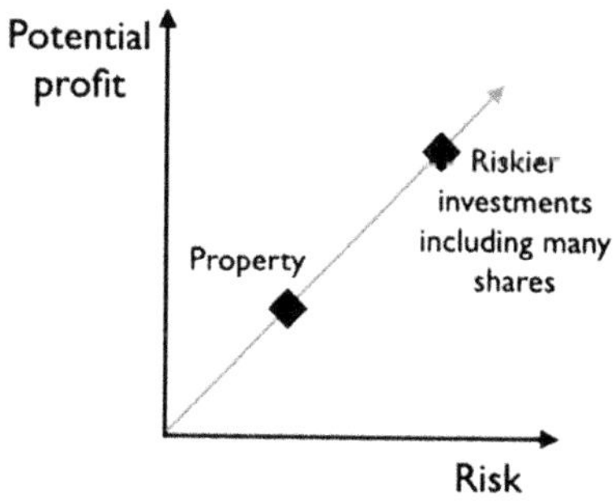

Figure 2.2: Property offers a lower (better) risk/reward ratio than opportunities offering higher potential returns, with higher variability and less stability, including many shares.

Example: A 90% probability of a 10% return gives a 9% risk-weighted return. A 50% probability of a 10% return gives a 5% risk-weighted return. The first of these offers a better risk/reward ratio. There is a lower chance of not achieving the return: a lower risk/reward and a higher risk-weighted return.

Explanation: In the UK, strong residential property market returns are underpinned by a relatively fixed supply and growing demand. We all need a roof over our heads, regardless of the economy. Rental properties are especially attractive. This is because rents don't tend to fluctuate in response to macroeconomic changes so much and profits do not depend on sustained housing market gains. There is also a strong legal framework and enforcement. This reduces risks, as well as the correlation with other asset classes and external changes. There is both downside protection and a low risk/reward ratio. A low risk/reward ratio is the panacea for investors.

HOW HARD IT WILL BE: THE EFFORT YOU HAVE TO PUT IN AND EFFORT/REWARD RATIO

> ***Definition:*** *This relates to how easy an opportunity is. How much effort, time, money and expertise are needed for a given return?*

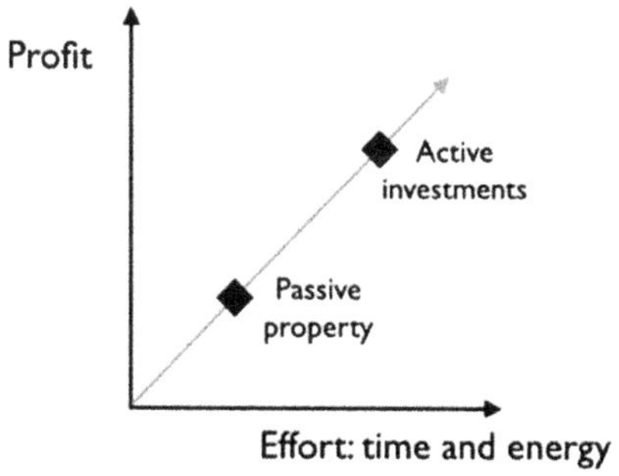

Figure 2.3: Passive property investments (e.g. shares in REITs) and semi-passive property investments (e.g. long-term, well-managed properties requiring no work) generally offer a better effort/reward ratio than active investments (e.g. trading shares or buying a property to renovate and sell).

Example 1: Let's say you can make a 5% passive return each year through a long-term investment. This might compare well for investors with limited time against a 20% return that requires a more active approach. The active return requires more effort: overseeing transactions or even being on-site every week to check-in on the builders. When you're assessing an opportunity, it is not just about a return on funds, but a return on time and energy.

Example 2: The same ratio can be extended to other resources. If it takes one year versus ten years to save for an investment, the effort is much lower. At this point, it's worth mentioning borrowing, as a way to leverage capital.

Let's say, a block of flats is worth £1,000,000 and you can achieve a net rental income of £60,000 after all the property and management costs have been taken into account.

Purchase price	£1,000,000
Net income	£60,000
Net yield (net return on investment per annum for a cash only deal)	6%
Deposit	£250,000
Loan to value	75%
Loan amount	£750,000
Interest rate	3.50%
Interest per annum	£26,250
Income after finance costs per annum	£33,750
Return on investment per annum	13.50%

Figure 2.4 - The power of leverage is illustrated by how net income after all costs divided by the equity required to do the deal is improved with borrowing. In this example, the annual income would improve from 6% to 13.5%.

You can enhance your returns because the cost of finance is less than the rental yield. Fewer resources and less effort are required to achieve the same profit level.

Explanation: Political encouragement, notably under Thatcher, and a historically light-touch regulatory environment have made both homeownership and property investment relatively easy in the UK. Increased availability of buy-to-let mortgages from 1997 reduced financial barriers to investing. Less capital and, therefore, less effort were required. Smaller investors were able to quickly buy up properties, which often required relatively modest savings for deposits, to build a rental portfolio. The opportunity to leverage returns, financially and in relation to other resources, created substantial growth in the demand for investment properties.

It appeared that pretty much anyone could build a buy-to-let portfolio on the side of their career or business. Being a property investor was seen as totally accessible and a relatively easy way to create and preserve wealth.

A proliferation of businesses that market specific property-related opportunities as products have continued to make investing easier. There are consumer-friendly finance options through to glossy brochures and comfy marketing suites outlining off-plan acquisitions.

It's no surprise that the private rental sector (PRS) became dominated by typically smaller private investors. By 2016, over 60% of private UK landlords owned just one rental property. Only 7% of landlords owned five properties or more. Many buy-to-let investors were accidental landlords. Often they fell into property through inheritance or lifestyle changes, such as moving in with a partner who also owned a property.[10]

WHAT YOU ARE MISSING OUT ON: THE OPPORTUNITY COST

> **Definition:** *The financial opportunity cost of capital is what your money could be earning through alternatives, such as other types of investment or savings mechanisms. It is about comparing returns from one opportunity with the returns available through others.*

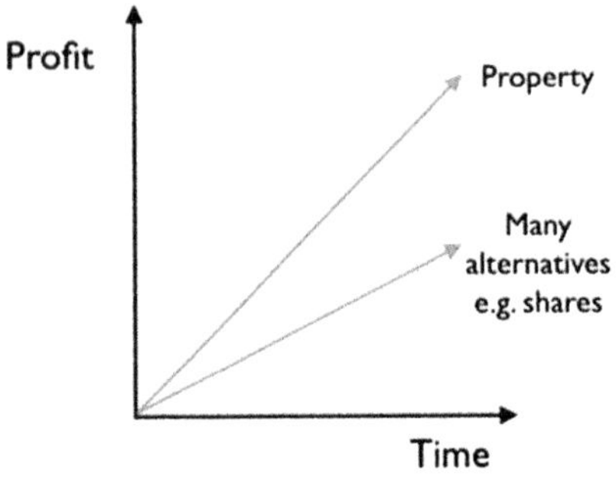

Figure 2.5: Property has performed well compared with many alternatives in recent years.

Example: A 5% return seems very attractive against the alternatives, delivering 1% each year. The same 5% return is hardly appealing if the alternatives are delivering 10% per annum.

Explanation: UK residential property has performed well compared with the alternatives that are available to many ordinary investors. Even before leverage is taken into account, it beat the stock market, bonds and cash between 1955-2016.[11] However, the stock market fluctuates daily, so such comparisons rely heavily on when they are made.

At this point, it's worth mentioning how the alternatives to long-term rental properties in the UK residential sector have fared. The most common 'opportunity costs' in the property landscape to some form of professional private rental sector investment are outlined below, along with commentary on the associated returns, risks and effort:

Private landlord buy-to-let – this performed very well until regulatory changes began to discourage private individuals from owning a small handful of rental investments, from 2015. Since then, it has generally only been considered a good idea for investors who prefer not to invest with leverage on their portfolios due to tax changes, which I will explain later.

Residential development – this has offered very strong returns, with capital growth allowing investors to smooth over any errors in many parts of the country for over twenty years. That is, until the raft of regulatory changes previously mentioned, notably the Stamp Duty Land Tax Surcharge. This has made residential development into a high effort, high-risk approach with uncertain returns as costs are higher and revenues less certain.

Commercial investment – this typically offers relatively strong yields that are fixed for a long time and require very little effort. However, specialist knowledge is required, so making the right decisions is harder. Further, valuations are determined by covenant strength. Money can be made or lost quickly due to who you rent to, how credible they are and what level of security is offered. A change in your tenants' businesses can change the value of your investment overnight. Political change, such as Brexit-related uncertainty, or economic and social changes catalysed by Covid-19 can easily wipe millions off a portfolio value through no fault of your own as an investor.

Ground rents – historically, these rents have offered very secure long-term income for investors able to understand the sometimes complicated legal frameworks surrounding owning the freehold and leasing out flats, typically in a multi-unit flat block. The current political will does not favour greedy freeholders and ground rents are now limited by policy direction from the Government and banks, making this form of investment less profitable. Effort is very low, but the regulatory risk is high.

Student housing – this has been historically popular with both private and institutional investors. Due to its popularity, supply and demand dynamics have been thrown off course in many areas. Thousands of fancy new units have been built simultaneously, meaning more competition and lower returns. Risks are related to what happens in the local and national tertiary education sector. The effort required is similar to the effort needed in other parts of the rental property market; however, as competition has increased, returns have reduced.

Later living – a very popular area for institutions as the direction of demographic changes means demand is growing for this type of housing. However, both specialist knowledge and scale are required, and as with student housing, the future supply and demand dynamics are not yet clear as a lot of supply is in the pipeline. Thousands of units are currently in progress, which will drive down returns in the future. Substantial management effort is required.

Build to Rent – this is a very small portion of the wider private rental sector (<3% at the time of writing), yet this specialism has received substantial attention. One issue is that supply and demand are finely balanced and the addition of hundreds of often premium units in a small market could mean lower returns than forecast for many of these schemes.

Further, the cost bases are much higher than for buying and perhaps refurbishing existing units. Build to Rent is riskier and requires more effort than many investors have openly discussed, as there is a high level of development risk and uncertainty about future returns due to planning and construction time lags and potential local oversupply.

Houses in Multiple Occupancy (HMOs) – traditionally, HMOS offered higher yields as having, for example, five tenants in a single house, with each paying a room rent, gives a higher gross income. They attract both individuals and institutions from an investment perspective and, in many areas, supply exceeds demand. The regulatory compliance and management burden is higher. They require a lot of effort and are considered to be relatively risky due to all the things that could go wrong with multiple tenants in one building.

STRATEGY SOUNDBITE CHAPTER SUMMARY

Long-term UK residential property investment can deliver strong returns with low variability. Historically, it has been seen as more accessible, less effort, and lower risk than many of the alternatives, as well as able to deliver better returns. Many investors have been able to build up multi-million-pound portfolios and generate substantial profits on the side of their business or career. It's no surprise that residential property investment attracts interest from all walks of life. For many years, it seemed almost too good to be true.

CHAPTER 3

How the property market has changed, and why what worked before won't work any more

In this chapter, I will highlight what has changed in the UK residential property market over the last few years and how this new market context means that what once worked may no longer be viable for many investors.

It's not all doom and gloom, however. The fundamental forces of supply and demand have not changed. We all still need to live somewhere and supply is inevitably restricted. We have limited land, building constraints and a restrictive planning system. What investors want and need has not changed either. Investors still love the idea of stability, ongoing profits, and a way to grow wealth safely without too much effort.

However, market shifts have undeniably affected what works and how. These changes are beyond the control of any one investor. They affect the returns, risks, effort and performance relative to the alternatives that I outlined in the previous chapter. This is especially significant for private small and medium-sized (SME) investors.

As mentioned previously, most residential investors are small landlords with four or fewer properties (93% in 2016, though this percentage has fallen since).[12]

Many are unaware of some or all of the changes that are affecting them. Significantly, there is an overriding policy shift meaning that investors who want to continue investing profitably must scale up and professionalise or focus on indirect investments.

At the risk of dating this book, this chapter summarises what's changed in recent years across six key areas: political, economic, social, technological, legal/regulatory and environmental.

It's important to understand these changes before you invest as they will affect your outcomes and decisions.

1. POLITICAL CHANGES: EXAGGERATING, BUT NOT CAUSING A SLOWDOWN

When I began writing this book, the impact of Brexit was the first question investors asked me about. There was huge uncertainty that stretched out for years. What would happen, how, and when? Question marks around Brexit created a less confident environment and delayed decisions, resulting in reduced supply of new housing stock, lower valuations and slower sales cycles.

Newspaper headlines suggested that political uncertainty was the cause of housing market doom. Contrary to popular opinion, the evidence suggested otherwise. Uncertainty had the effect of compounding existing property market issues, rather than causing them.[13]

Since then, confidence has improved in line with greater political certainty. So why keep commentary on this particular political shift in the book? The truth is, regardless of the realities of implementing Brexit, this will not be the last cause of political change and uncertainty our property market experiences, and it's not over yet. In fact, between drafting and publishing this book, the world began to feel the economic, social, health and political consequences of Covid-19, again highlighting how such crises and uncertainty can affect short- to medium-term confidence.

Long-term investors must remember one key point. Markets and opportunists can be forgetful. This point is relevant whether the question of the day is around Brexit uncertainties, pandemics, or uncertainties created by any other issue. The long-term performance of residential property investment is driven by long-term demand for, and supply of, housing. The structural causes of demand and supply for housing are not really affected by any short-term uncertainty. In the absence of structural change, the growing demand for affordable, quality housing and a shortage of supply continues.

Demand for housing is essential in nature. This is evidenced by how Brexit uncertainties had a negligible impact on residential property rental demand, though they have affected valuations and the demand for housing.

Meanwhile, housing supply is relatively fixed and slow to respond. This is what economists describe as 'inelastic'. Research suggests we need 340,000 new homes built annually up to 2031.[14] We remain woefully below that level of new supply, as an average of only 122,704 new homes were completed each year between 2010 and 2017.[15] Affordability constraints mean there is continued and growing demand for rental properties from tenants. New regulations, tax frameworks affecting second-time buyers and tighter lending criteria introduced by banks are restricting new supply from investors.

The shortage of well-managed, quality, affordable housing in areas where people want and need to live is a political issue that affects the housing market more significantly than Brexit. Political uncertainty can clearly exaggerate issues by affecting confidence. However, it is not the underlying cause of structural property market changes.

2. ECONOMIC CHANGES: INCREASING DEMAND FROM TENANTS AND INVESTORS

The economy has a big impact on investment. Yet demand for housing has a relatively low correlation to economic demand, as we all need a roof over our heads. This is one of the most attractive things about investing in residential property.

Important trends relating to our economy include long-term low interest rates[16] that continue to stimulate property demand. Capital is easily available and investors have a strong demand for yields that exceed the base rate. This low base rate environment is likely to stay. Reasons for this include how technological improvements inspire greater efficiency and this is keeping inflation levels low. It also means base rates cannot be reduced by much to stimulate investment or consumption.

As a result, the idea that growth in investor appetites will continue to result in blanket capital growth seems unlikely.

Thanks to globalisation, strong rewards and low risks, capital continues to be attracted into the UK property market. At the time of writing, UK property assets are discounted internationally, thanks to the weak value of the pound, itself a factor of confidence and interest rates. Consequently, international demand and, therefore, property values remain relatively stable.

There are plenty of reasons why owner-occupiers, national and international investors continue to be attracted to UK property. It is still a great asset for investors seeking returns and stability. Competition from powerful institutions, international investors, and other income-hungry investors is bidding prices up for income-focused assets, such as student housing. This, in turn, pushes yields down.

3. SOCIAL CHANGES: GROWING DEMAND FOR AFFORDABLE, QUALITY HOUSING AND GROWING DEMAND FOR YIELD-FOCUSED INVESTMENT

Population growth, demographic changes and preferences mean there are more smaller households and a higher demand for housing.

The number of families in the UK increased by 8% in the ten years to 2018. Household sizes are shrinking, compounded by a higher divorce rate and healthcare improvements that mean people are living longer.[17] When this is combined with rising living standards and a preference for smaller households, it results in a higher demand for housing. This has pushed prices and rents up.

Affordability is constraining homeownership and investment, particularly for the younger generation. Average house prices have risen from being around five times higher than people's income in 2002 to almost eight times by 2018.[18] 'Generation Rent' struggle to get on the housing ladder, as a result.

In 2018, the average single first-time buyer needed ten years to save a 15% deposit for a property (and significantly longer in London).[19] It's no surprise that in the twenty years to 2018, the proportion of younger people (25-34) owning their own home fell from 48% to 28%.[20] More broadly, millennials are settling down later and increasingly favour flexible access to premium features, such as a concierge or gym, over the less affordable and less flexible responsibility and burden of property ownership. The trend of access over ownership[21] encompasses transport, for example, using Uber rather than owning a car, through to housing. Younger people are less likely to buy, as homeowners or investors, and more likely to rent. Continued and growing demand for rental housing improves the potential returns to well-located, well-priced long-term property investments.

On the investment side, one consequence of the preference for access over ownership is how many retiring landlords are facing succession issues. 60% of the landlord population is aged over 55.[22] Since more than 90% of the UK's private rental sector housing stock is owned by private landlords, this is a substantial force.

Our ageing population also creates more competition for yield-focused investments. Pension funds are becoming the most powerful investors globally in absolute and relative terms, and have a growing appetite for stable, income-producing assets. The requirement for yield from these powerful, sophisticated investors has been exaggerated thanks to compulsory pension contributions.[23]

4. TECHNOLOGICAL CHANGES: MAKING INVESTING MORE ACCESSIBLE

Technology is opening up access in the property market, as well as increasing efficiency and quality for cost. Proptech has grown exponentially in its impact, often at little or no cost to the user. Online listing portals, such as Zoopla and Rightmove, have opened up access to opportunities and data. More digitised processes, such as Customer Relationship Management software, are making management easier, cheaper and faster. Digital and online booking capabilities, like Airbnb, enable homeowners to flexibly rent out space and mean that people can move around more easily. The growing impact of online and hybrid estate agencies and lettings services, data platforms and the tokenisation of real estate through alternative finance are improving accessibility to specific opportunities and information.

We are moving into an age where data-driven decisions can be made with limited human interference. Investors can find, research and manage opportunities and implement decisions from anywhere in the world. Investing can be as easy as shopping on eBay, via crowdfunding or peer-to peer-loan platforms.

5. LEGAL AND REGULATORY CHANGE: SHIFTING THE BALANCE OF POWER FROM SMALLER INVESTORS

Legal and regulatory factors are perhaps the most important cause of change in the UK property market. There is cross-party political will to solve the housing crisis and professionalise property investment. The increased cost and administrative burden of staying on top of more regulations discourage small investors with a few buy-to-lets. Armchair investment is becoming less profitable, more challenging and more time-consuming.

Regulatory and legal considerations for property investors include:

- Changes to Mortgage Interest Relief via Section 24, which have increased the tax burden for individuals owning buy-to-let property. Holding a property with a mortgage for a higher or nearly higher rate taxpayer has shifted from being a profitable sideline business to a real loss. If mortgage interest was 75%+ of rental income on a property before this change, the new regime means the investor owning this property in their personal name will now begin to make a loss.[24]

- The Stamp Duty Land Tax (SDLT) surcharge, an additional 3% on top of the existing transaction tax, makes buying more residential properties less attractive. With the surcharge, SDLT would be £9,000 rather than £2,100 on a purchase price of £230,000 (about the average for UK properties).

- New lending standards from the Prudential Regulation Authority have caused friction on the financing side. For landlords with four or more properties, borrowing is now harder.

- Additional licensing requirements mean that strong and specialist local and national market knowledge is required by investors. There are more and more stringent local and national regulations. These range from national House in Multiple Occupancy (HMO) licensing to the Selective Licensing of private rental properties in specific geographies.

- The Tenant Fees Act 2019 has shifted costs from the tenant to investors, meaning that traditional buy-to-let investments have lower returns.

- Other taxes, such as the Annual Tax on Enveloped Dwellings, add to the cost base and administrative burden of property investment in company structures.

- Meanwhile, tax reliefs, such as for Build to Rent (scaled development for the purpose of holding long-term to rent out), or Real Estate Investment Trusts (REITs), which are funds focused on holding property, make institutional investment easier and mean it's harder for smaller investors to compete.

A combination of political will across parties and recent regulations is encouraging professional, institutional investment. By contrast, homeownership is the only form of direct ownership that individuals are encouraged towards, in particular first-time buyers and those who do not own a home. The idea behind professionalisation is that fewer larger and more professional operators are easier to regulate and oversee to ensure professional standards and better housing opportunities for all. The days when slum landlords made easy money without taking care of their tenants are over.

The increased cost and administrative burden of staying on top of more regulations mean that traditional approaches to property are less profitable, more challenging and more time-consuming. Private property investors are being discouraged from direct investments. Instead, they are being encouraged to focus on the increasing range of truly passive property investment options. Individual investors facing shrinking profit margins are offloading thousands of privately-owned rental properties.

These changes are significant for people who intend to invest, as well as for the housing market because smaller investors dominate the market. Across the market, the proportion of landlords with just one property has declined from 78% in 2010 to 45% in 2018. The proportion of landlords with five or more properties has increased from 5% to 17% and is still rising. Many small investors who are aware of these market-wide changes are scaling up, professionalising or getting out.[25]

6. ENVIRONMENTAL CHANGES: THE GROWING IMPORTANCE OF ENVIRONMENTAL SUSTAINABILITY

Globally, Environmental Social and Governance (ESG) investing is now worth $30 trillion in Assets Under Management each year, around a quarter of all professionally managed assets. It's more relevant now than ever as the 'high impact, low probability' shock imposed by Covid-19 has strengthened the case for prioritising people and planet alongside profits, and illustrated the power of collective action to tackle global problems.

The UK's legally binding commitment to achieve Net Carbon Zero by 2050 means that sustainability is no longer a 'nice to have'. Our legal obligation is showing up in the form of new rules, regulations and best practices affecting all sectors that contribute to emissions.

Many property investors are unaware of how significant this trend will be for them through the 2020s. On the environmental side of ESG investing, there are two key areas of risk that will affect investor values and returns through the 2020s and beyond. Firstly, there's physical 'climate risk', for example the risk of flooding in areas of coastal erosion. Secondly, there is 'transition risk' for a significant proportion of our housing stock, which will need to be improved in order to align with the direction of political and social will.

The reality is, 40% of UK emissions come from households,[26] and over 75% of UK housing stock was built before building regulations required insulation.[27]

As a result, further regulations and policies designed to improve the environmental performance of residential property are more likely than not. These new regulations will not only affect your ability to operate in a way that is compliant, but they are likely to fundamentally change the value, performance and risk associated with your investments.

STRATEGY SOUNDBITE: CHAPTER SUMMARY

The fundamental forces of supply and demand have not changed. We all still need to live somewhere, and housing supply is inevitably restricted in the UK. What investors want and need has not changed either. Investors still love the idea of stability, ongoing profits, and a way to grow wealth safely, without too much effort.

Currently, the vast majority of UK property investors lack knowledge of some or all of the trends described in this chapter. The impacts of these six key areas of change are unavoidable and inevitable. Regulatory changes, in particular, have affected the viability of traditionally profitable approaches to UK residential property and increased the costs and risks of getting it wrong. Traditional approaches to UK residential property, such as sideline buy-to-let investment, are more costly and complicated for the type of investor who has come to dominate the private rental sector.

TAKEAWAY TIPS

To invest successfully in this new environment you must understand this fast-changing market, and then ensure your approach is strategic, value-focused, professional and sustainable. For many would-be armchair investors, this means taking a step back, focusing on the fundamentals of demand and supply, and targeting truly passive options led by professional operators rather than taking a hands-on role. Far from being bad news, greater complexity and uncertainty creates opportunity, and the opportunities for many investors today are a better fit for what they really want and need: passive, relatively low-risk investments.

For further updates on the impacts of new regulatory and wider market changes, I regularly share updates and insights which you can access for free. Connect on LinkedIn (https://www.linkedin.com/in/annaclareharper/), join my mailing list (https://annaclareharper.com/contact/) and download or listen to The Return: Property & Investment Podcast on iTunes, Spotify or online (bit.ly/returnpodcast).

CHAPTER 4

Why it's still a great time to invest, if you know what works

In this chapter, I'll share how investors can think in new ways to sidestep the challenges and make the most of opportunities. I'll explain why it is important for investors to take a more strategic, value-focused, professional and sustainable approach. I'll also share some ideas about what this means in practice.

Market changes and uncertainties have created problems. They have also opened up new opportunities, in particular for investors who, ideally, want to be passive and invest on the side.

A MORE STRATEGIC APPROACH

We need to be smarter about how we invest. The risks and costs associated with making emotional or wrong decisions have grown. A more complex and uncertain market means the cushioning effect of a buoyant market is no longer guaranteed.

Being strategic is about focusing on moving towards a goal. It requires you to understand your starting point, endgame and the market context. It requires you to make rational decisions and rely on facts and fundamentals rather than luck. It is about being decisive, rather than delaying or avoiding making decisions.

I often hear from investors who wanted one thing and found themselves going after another. For example, they say they have no spare time and then focus on active, direct investments. If your starting point is having no spare time then the right opportunities for you will be passive. This generally means taking a hands-off approach: indirect investments.

Other investors say they really want financial freedom and then invest in short-term, speculative development projects. If the goal is financial freedom, safety and security, then this means focusing on yield and opportunities that will stand the test of time.

A MORE PROFESSIONAL APPROACH

Regulations designed to make the residential property market more professional add to the investors' burden. More effort is required to make the same level of profit in a way that is legal, compliant and, therefore, sustainable. Opportunities that could have been financed and run by an individual or family have become less attractive. They are less profitable and more hassle. The cross-party political will that is in favour of a more professional environment encourages investors to scale up, get out or specialise in the role of investing.

It is important to return to the fact that market fundamentals remain strong. Regardless of what changes are affecting the property landscape, demand for housing is not likely to fall any time soon. It continues to grow against a backdrop of relatively fixed supply. UK residential property is poised to remain a strong asset class. It still offers a solution to investors seeking ongoing rewards as a way to preserve and grow wealth for the future.

However, it no longer makes sense for investors to use their old familiar approaches. At the time of writing, more than 90% of investors still hold stock inefficiently in their personal names.

The solution is not just about buying property in a company name rather than your personal name. This adds administrative demands and reporting and is generally not worthwhile unless you plan to build a substantial portfolio. Both the cost and complexity of complying with more consumer-friendly regulations affect investors in any structure. It also increases the chances of getting it wrong through non-compliance. For investors who are restricted by geography, it is more important to have trusted on-the-ground teams and specific local and national market knowledge. This includes international investors attracted by the stability of the UK property market.

The regulatory burden designed to make housing more professional means that it makes sense for many investors to scale up or get out of direct residential property investment and instead focus on indirect opportunities, which offer genuinely passive returns.

If you see yourself as an investor then it increasingly makes sense to specialise in financing investments. The operator then specialises in running things, becoming more efficient and consumer-focused.

In many ways, UK property investing is becoming more like investing in companies. Ownership and control are being separated. Rather than blurred lines, there are clearer parameters guiding the responsibilities and payoffs to ownership and control.

Thanks to technology and growing sophistication there are plenty of exciting opportunities. More of these are genuinely passive, so they are better suited to investors with funding but limited time. In this digital age, passive property investing can be as quick and easy as online shopping. Options to invest passively include via:

- Private Equity funds.
- Public investments, for example, shareholders owning residential property via listed real estate funds, such as REITs.
- Specific joint venture projects, for example, Special Purpose Vehicles through which a High Net Worth investor funds a deal or portfolio.
- Crowdfunding or peer to peer platforms, through which private investors can fund parts of different portfolios and projects.

The role of the financier has been important in the property world for many years. Property investing is capital intensive and can require, attract and generate a lot of money. Specialising in the role of the financier means minimal investor involvement. This is no bad thing. If you choose to go down this route, you can focus on structuring and selecting the right opportunities, rather than focusing on specific properties. For example, different platforms or funds to invest with. You can focus on improving your risk-adjusted returns through diversifying.

By working with specialists you can often access opportunities which you may not have access to on your own.

Many professionals in the sector make the most of this to get access to opportunities they would not otherwise have the chance to invest in. They take a passive role in carefully selected projects or platforms and leverage the work of others. This is something many of the investors I've worked with have wanted to do.

FOCUS ON VALUE

The importance of understanding value rather than just price has increased in this challenging, changing market. In the words of Warren Buffet:

> *"It's only when the tide goes out that you discover who's been swimming naked."*

This vividly illustrates how a buoyant market cushions and conceals mistakes.

In a bull market, you might be able to buy an overpriced property and rely on capital growth to smooth things out. In an uncertain, slow market, it's not safe to rely on capital growth to make things right.

Royal Institution of Chartered Surveyors (RICS) define value as:

> *'...the estimated amount for which a property should exchange on the date of valuation between a willing buyer and a willing seller in an arm's length transaction after proper marketing, wherein the parties had acted knowledgeably, prudently and without compulsion'.*

Value investing in the UK residential property market is about more than this. Warren Buffet's thesis of value investing is about investing in assets with strong long-term fundamentals. You buy assets when they are well-priced and hold them into the future:

"…our favourite holding period is forever."

This applies to property as it does to other forms of investment, like stocks and shares.

I have come to believe the best approaches to investing centre on more than just quick profits. Instead, they resolve real problems, enable investors to achieve sustainable returns, create social value and leave a lasting positive legacy. Assets with strong fundametals deliver ongoing, sustainable returns because they solve market problems, for example, providing safe, quality housing for people who want and need to live in a specific area at a price they can afford. If the problem is non-cyclical, then value is more likely to hold through cycles. This means you can access income and growth and make attractive returns, and it means you can have a positive impact on the communities you invest in, in any market.

The number of homeless people living on the streets is a visible reminder of one of the big problems in the UK residential property market. There is a shortage of quality, affordable housing where people want and need to live. Solving issues like this is a great way to access value regardless of what is happening in the market.

As for timing, the advice of Warren Buffet, who you may notice is my favourite investor to quote, seems relevant again:

"...when others are fearful, be greedy."

Much of the stock owned by traditional landlords still benefits from strong fundamentals. It meets market needs by providing relatively affordable housing in the places where people want and need to live.

On supply: the number of households renting in England more than doubled in the last decade and the number of new households created annually is almost twice the number of new dwellings being built. By any standard, there is clearly a huge, unmet and growing demand for housing that people can afford to live in. Consequently, tenant demand is strong and rising.

On affordability: housing is considered 'affordable' (with a lower case 'a') if the cost of living is less than 35% of median incomes in the area. This kind of housing is in short supply. As a result, the government has stepped in. In an effort to resolve the shortage of affordable housing, developers are mandated to provide 'Affordable' (with a capitalised 'A') housing on new developments.

If you are investing directly, then you need to consider how your approach allows you to access (and deliver) value. If you are investing indirectly as a passive investor then you need to look at the investment strategy of the provider or platform you are considering investing with. Do they focus on prime housing that's suitable for wealthy international students? Or do they provide housing that workers in local hospitals or Amazon warehouses can afford to live in?

A MORE SUSTAINABLE APPROACH

For investors, the traditional goal of profit maximisation is being replaced. To align with the times we are in, and the direction of political will, investments must increasingly be sustainable as well as profitable: economically resilient, with positive ESG metrics.

So how can property investors approach their investments in a way that is sustainable, as well as profitable?

Compliance with current and anticipated regulatory changes is a helpful baseline for a sustainable approach, because the UK government is proactive in its pursuit of sustainability via regulations.

For now, the greatest regulatory pressure relates to the environmental performance of buildings. This means that the first and most important step is to understand the environmental performance, costs and risks associated with your portfolio and future acquisitions. The reality is, the cost of 'retrofitting' older, less environmentally-friendly properties can be high, whether or not you are able to use subsidies and grants designed to support the transition to a greener housing market.

One of the main ways to measure environmental sustainability is Energy Performance Certificate (EPC) ratings. There are already regulations around these that affect property values and rentability. Since 1 April 2018, it has been illegal to grant a new tenancy on properties with an EPC rating of below E. Since 1 April 2020, it has been illegal to continue letting such property (unless exempted).[28] This minimum standard is expected to increase over the coming years, and it is likely that EPC ratings will impact your ability to mortgage properties too, as the UK government strives to meet its legally binding commitment to achieve Net Carbon Zero.

A good practical starting point is to focus on properties that are environmentally efficient, or that are easy and cheap to upgrade. You should consider environmental efficiency in pre-planned maintenance schedules at the time of acquisition, or when reviewing your portfolio.

It also makes sense to keep an eye on, and be ready to adopt innovations in the sector which will make better environmental performance cheaper and easier, from air quality sensors to smart meters

The direction of government regulations creates little doubt that environmental performance will impact your ability to sell or rent out properties. Less environmentally friendly properties will increasingly be worth less, and be less able to deliver cash flow. Greener properties will increasingly be worth more, and hold their value better. So, if you're not already considering how to factor in sustainability when you review your current portfolio and next acquisitions, in particular in terms of environmental performance, you need to do so now or work with someone who can support you with this.

STRATEGY SOUNDBITE
CHAPTER SUMMARY

The fundamentals underlying residential property have not changed. It can still deliver sustainable, ongoing profits. It is still a great time to invest. However, new regulations and market dynamics have particularly affected outcomes for smaller investors, who must be more strategic, focused, professional and sustainable in their approach.

For many would-be armchair investors, this new environment means not taking a hands-on role. Instead, it might involve partnering with joint-venture operators, investing in listed property vehicles, or investing via alternative finance platforms. What to invest in and when to do this is unique to each investor.

The methodology provided later in this book will help you to define your personal approach. The headline is this: for many passive, funded investors, direct ownership is less attractive now.

The good news is, there are more genuinely passive options available than ever, offering easier rewards with greater confidence.

CHAPTER 5

What doesn't work? Seven common, expensive mistakes to avoid

In this chapter, I'll dig into what happens if you don't take the right approach and highlight seven common, expensive investor mistakes.

As I've already outlined, residential property investing by traditional direct methods is no longer the bullseye it used to be. We live in an era of uncertainty and increasing regulation. There is a downside and greater chance of pitfalls associated with avoidable errors.

For the types of investor I work with, who have access to substantial funding, a poor decision can equate to multi-million-pound losses. So, it's worth being aware of the potential pitfalls. This chapter highlights what happens when you don't invest in the right way. It shares common expensive mistakes I've witnessed investors make which relate to the three essentials of property investing: strategy, deals and management. The methodology in the following part of this book will help you to avoid making mistakes like these.

1. STRATEGIC MISTAKES

Firstly, there are three expensive strategic mistakes that result directly from not having a clear, suitable strategy:

Expensive Mistake 1: making emotional decisions

Property can be emotive. It is all too easy to get carried away and fall into traps if you go after shiny objects, follow the herd or follow your heart. Emotional decisions wilfully ignore realities and rationality. A more strategic approach is a great way to protect yourself against potential traps.

Expensive Mistake 2: diving in or dithering

In an age of distraction and busy-ness, we're all short on time. Some people react to this overwhelm by diving in before they have done enough research. This can be the result of assuming it will be easy or being enthusiastic to get started. The flip side to diving in is dithering. Through fear, ditherers will over-analyse and delay. In this digital age, it's becoming easier to do research before taking action. Desktop research can be a great help. It is also easier to find fault with every opportunity, which creates plenty of excuses not to invest.

Expensive Mistake 3: relying on trends

Trends create headlines. Extrapolating from headlines can oversimplify matters with potentially expensive consequences.

For example, investors might allocate capital based on historic rather than current market drivers. As a result, they may over- or under-invest in specific niches or areas.

How to avoid expensive strategic mistakes

For all of the three mistakes linked to strategy, there's a common theme: not following a clear strategy.

You need to step back from the risks of irrational decision-making by setting your strategy first. This requires you to look at your goal, starting point and relevant market realities, and then map out an effective path.

There is no right answer to the question of what strategy to take. However, there are huge benefits from having a path to follow, from starting point to end goal, taking into account the market and your own circumstances.

2. DEAL-RELATED MISTAKES

Deals are closely connected to and defined by strategy.

The following mistakes result from poor management of deals:

Expensive Mistake 4: mistaking price for value and misunderstanding costs

It is often assumed that if the price of a property is discounted, it will be a better deal. In many cases, price does not reflect true market value. It often has little bearing on how well a property investment will hold its value long-term. Further, many investors misunderstand or inadvertently minimise costs in a subconscious attempt to make the deal work.

Expensive Mistake 5: misunderstanding timing

There's always some reason to feel like it might be better to wait or why it's too late. Many potential investors miss out on returns because they've misunderstood market or personal timing. The right decision at the wrong time is often still the wrong decision.

Lengthy transaction processes mean that acquiring property often takes longer than anticipated. The process of negotiating, conveyancing and arranging finance always seems to take longer than the investor would like.

Expensive Mistake 6: speculating

All too often, investors confuse high potential returns for high actual returns. Unproven projects will not necessarily deliver the best profit once they are adjusted for risk. Investors in speculative projects can end up taking on huge risks, often without realising it. Examples include development projects or new build rental schemes with no track record for the forecast rent.

Ultimately, if it sounds too good to be true, it probably is.

How to avoid deal-related mistakes

Deal-related mistakes can relate to doing deals that don't align with your strategy. They can also be caused by market imperfections, particularly in relation to information. You need access to deals that suit your approach and the ability to assess them.

3. ASSET MANAGEMENT MISTAKES

Once a deal has been done, asset management of property investments is crucial. The final mistake relates to this:

Expensive Mistake 7: misunderstanding the realities

Before they invest, some people see property as it is portrayed in the media: relatively easy and accessible. This can lead them to invest too readily, on the assumption that they won't need to put much effort in. Others see it as too hard and believe that it's not possible because they don't have the time, resources or connections to invest in a complex market. Both these mistakes are caused by misunderstanding what it takes. It is possible. What often needs to change is the approach and the assumption that the only way to invest is as a direct investor acting alone.

How to avoid asset management mistakes

You need the ability to manage assets in a way that is profitable, professional, consumer-focused and compliant in this more complicated environment. This requires you to understand the effort required, as well as how and when to work with others.

STRATEGY SOUNDBITE CHAPTER SUMMARY

The most common, expensive mistakes result from the lack of three things:

1. *A clear strategy suited to the investor, their goals, situation and the market*
2. *The right deal criteria, a well-managed deal pipeline and quality transactions*
3. *Strong professional asset management.*

The truth is, not having these three things in place is likely to cause investors more pain than ever.

We are in new uncharted waters. Investing directly in residential property is not as easy as it once was. Investors need to understand and navigate a complicated environment. The soft landing of a buoyant market has been paved over. The rosy glow of a buy-to-let boom has been dimmed down, leading to a greater likelihood of getting things wrong and at a greater cost. To avoid common, expensive mistakes, you need to know what doesn't work.

PART 2

Investing

SECTION I

Methodology

CHAPTER 6

A five-step methodology for investing in any market

In Part 1, I explained how residential property is not as easy as it once was. In this complex environment, with so many new regulations, many approaches that worked before are no longer viable.

In Part 2, I share a simple methodology you can use to define the right strategy for you in this more complex environment, rather than relying on luck.

This part of the book includes practical guidance around what I have come to believe are three essential components of residential property investing. These steps will maximise your chances of success and minimise the chances of making common expensive mistakes outlined earlier.

The three essentials are:

1. **A clear strategy suited to the investor, their goals, situation and the market**

2. **The right deal criteria, a well-managed deal pipeline and quality transactions**

3. **Strong, professional asset management.**

None of this is complicated on its own but there are plenty of people who don't get it right. They forget about strategy. They don't know how to manage their deal pipeline (a way to filter down opportunities and select the ones that seem the best) effectively, or don't have the capacity to do this. They don't have the resources to operate professionally. The sad truth is, without any one of these essentials, their success is likely to be cut short. All three are needed. Like a three-legged stool, without one, it all falls down.

The linchpin is having the right strategy.

This is what connects you today with where you want to be. It both defines and is defined by the other essentials. Investors who don't take a strategic perspective can fall into common traps. They might make emotional or speculative decisions and put capital at risk. In this complex environment, it has never been more important to define a clear strategy before you invest.

WHAT IS NEEDED TO DEFINE A CLEAR STRATEGY?

The methodology I will share synthesises what I have learned over the years, investing in buoyant and less favourable times, studying the market academically at Cambridge, and discussing market challenges and opportunities with experts in the field for my podcast.

The 5As methodology is designed to aid you to:

- Confidently navigate a complex UK property market.
- Easily and efficiently access opportunities, without wasting time, money or effort.
- Drive sustainable, value-driven rewards into the future.

None of the steps in the methodology is complex, yet they are easy to forget or sidestep. You would be surprised by how many people neglect them. If you are considering investing in UK property, reading through and considering these steps before you invest could save you a lot of heartaches and headaches.

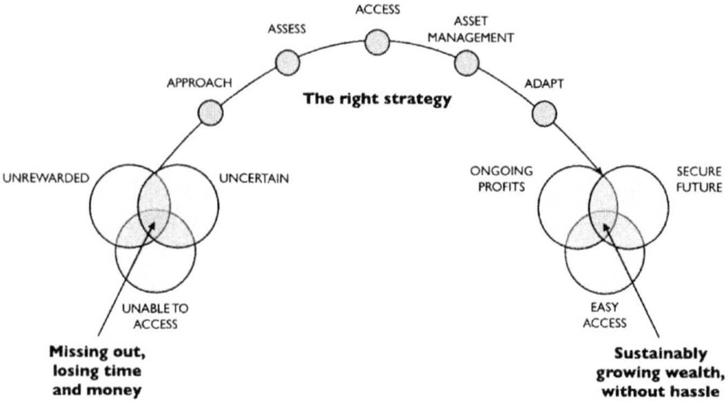

Figure 6.1: Investors need to consider each of the 5As to grow wealth and avoid missing out.

The 5As help you to:

- **Define a clear Approach**. This links back to your goals and available resources, as well as the current market context. It is about understanding what you are aiming to achieve, your starting point and how to logically connect the two.
- **Assess opportunities using clear criteria aligned with clear objectives.** Confidently filter down these opportunities and choose the ones that will move you closer to your specific goals.
- **More easily Access compelling opportunities.** Know how you are going to capitalise on opportunities that meet your criteria, then transact on these opportunities successfully.
- **Ensure Asset Management is done professionally and safely.** Enhance returns and minimise risks in an

increasingly regulated space. Make sure that your investments deliver what you want without hassle or huge personal time commitments.

- **Adapt to future market changes and trends, as required.** Know how and when to respond to future market changes.

Whilst Approach and Adapt embody strategy, Access, Assess and Asset Management relate more to implementation, feeding into and from strategy

APPROACH: WHAT APPROACH SHOULD YOU TAKE?

There are three key steps to answering this question:

1. **Start with the end in mind – set clear SMART goals.**
2. **Know your starting point in terms of time, money and industry expertise.**
3. **Find an efficient, effective and logical path between the two.**

Your strategy should suit the current market circumstances, your goals and your starting point. It should take into account rewards as well as risk, the effort required and available alternatives.

If you are looking to create income and preserve and grow your wealth, you'll want the investments to have a long-term focus. In this new market context, you need to structure things right. Holding properties in your personal name is generally no longer viable if you expect to have a mortgage. Meanwhile, setting up a company may be more hassle and cost than it's worth for a small portfolio. Accounting and administration costs can quickly run into thousands each year.

Consider your situation, tax circumstances, how quickly you might need your money (your liquidity preference) and your ability to invest directly. Are you happy to take on the responsibility of complying with new regulations?

Should you focus on a specific niche or diversify your funds across geographies, assets and tenant types to reduce exposure?

Increasingly, I see many investors preferring not to take a hands-on role. They prefer to partner with an operator, invest in listed property vehicles or invest via an alternative finance platform.

ASSESS: HOW ARE YOU GOING TO ASSESS OPPORTUNITIES?

To accurately assess opportunities, you need to use clear investment criteria aligned with your investment objectives. This involves the 6Ds.

D1: Deal Criteria aligned with your approach

You need clear criteria aligned with your objectives to know if an opportunity is right for you and will help move you closer to your goal. Many of the investors I work with, who are seeking a relatively low risk passive income, target an ongoing yield of 2-8%. If you take into account capital growth and choose to leverage your portfolio using debt finance, this can easily reach double digit annual returns.

D2: Diversity

Make sure your deal criteria allow you to diversify so that you don't end up 'over-exposed' to a particular approach or area.

D3: Due Diligence

Understand and consider costs and returns objectively through thorough due diligence.

D4: Decision-making

You need to be able to make decisions in line with your criteria, easily and objectively.

D5: Delegation and D6: Delivery Capabilities

When it comes to assessing opportunities, you can do the work yourself (Do It Yourself or DIY), seek some professional support (Done With You or DWY) or get someone to do the work for you (Done For You or DFY).

ACCESS: HOW ARE YOU GOING TO ACCESS OPPORTUNITIES THAT FIT WITH YOUR APPROACH?

You can more easily access compelling opportunities to invest that are suited to your investment criteria through three more steps relating to deals. These are:

1. **Have access to a strong pipeline of opportunities.**
2. **Have the ability to filter down.**
3. **Have the capability to manage quality transactions.**

Firstly, you need to have opportunities coming in so that you don't feel pressured to take up the first one you come across. This might be from an online source, the open market, or relationships.

Secondly, you need to be able to 'sort the wheat from the chaff'.

Thirdly, you need quality transactions. If you're looking at investing directly this will mean you need a suitable team to support you. Don't underestimate the value of a great conveyancing solicitor, with strong communication skills. Transactions also require administrative support and oversight to accelerate each opportunity.

Again, you need to decide if you want to Do It Yourself (DIY), have some professional support using a Done With You (DWY) service or have the work Done For You (DFY).

A key factor will be whether you have a strong understanding and set of contacts in the industry nationally and locally. If you're investing directly, do you have the contacts and local knowledge you will need in the places you want to invest? If not, who do you know who can help you so that you can minimise the chance of wasting time and money, or making expensive mistakes?

ASSET MANAGEMENT: HOW ARE YOU GOING TO ENSURE YOUR ASSETS ARE MANAGED PROFESSIONALLY AND SAFELY?

This has never been more important. Property investments must be managed professionally and safely to minimise risks in an increasingly regulated space. Asset management must be professional, profitable, and carried out in a consumer-focused, compliant way.

How are you going to make sure your investments deliver what you want if you prefer not to take on additional hassle, effort or time commitments? The answer may not be what it once was. Increasingly, I see investors focusing on choosing the right businesses to work with. Those businesses then focus on getting these things right. Asset management is important for enhancing returns and minimising risks. There are three steps you need to take:

1. Understand what needs to be done.
2. Understand how it can and should be done: professionally, profitably, and in a consumer-focused and compliant way.
3. Find the right person or team to do it: choose whether to DIY, DWY or DFY.

ADAPT: HOW WILL YOU ADAPT TO FUTURE MARKET CHANGES AND TRENDS?

Some investors just want to put money in and then, in the future, take more money out. For them, the idea of having to keep up with market trends and changes does not appeal. They just need to make sure they are ready and able to shift if the market changes at a structural level; for example, shifting to focus on yield rather than development profits.

Properties themselves are relatively illiquid, especially in a slower, less confident market. One way to ensure that you are ready to flex, if needed, is to focus on more liquid, easily accessible investments: shares in property investment businesses and funds. Shares can also be more favourable from a tax perspective, though you must seek tax advice on your circumstances.

To adapt, simply keep your eyes on the prize and decide when you will review, and pause, pivot or persevere.

STRATEGY SOUNDBITE CHAPTER SUMMARY

For investors with access to funding, three things are needed:

1. *A clear strategy suited to the investor, their goals, situation and the market*

2. *The right deal criteria aligned with that strategy, and quality transactions*

3. *Strong asset management.*

To ensure nothing gets left out, I've developed the 5As methodology. This covers approach, assessing and accessing deals, asset management, and adapting.

Whether you choose to be active or passive, this methodology can be used to help you to invest more strategically, successfully and safely in any market. It is designed to help you to answer the following question, which is so often asked:

"How can I invest in UK residential property to grow wealth safely, throughout market changes?"

SECTION 2

Strategy

CHAPTER 7

The three-step approach to creating a clear, logical and effective strategy

In this chapter, I'll explain why strategy is so important and briefly outline how to design a clear approach.

According to *The Oxford English Dictionary*, a strategy is:

> *"...a plan of action designed to achieve a long-term or overall aim."*

A well-designed property strategy is a way to help you achieve your goal easier, faster and more safely, avoiding expensive mistakes. It is a clear, logical, efficient path that takes into account current circumstances in the market and relevant circumstances for you as an investor. It helps with prioritising and allocating resources, especially as circumstances change. It can help you to reach the objective with less hassle and uncertainty, and more clarity at each decision point. For an investor, this greater efficiency and reduced risk is very attractive.

Strategy is important for all scales of investor. However simple it may sound, it's not easy to define a strategy or to stick to one. There's plenty of evidence of this. Highly successful global businesses still pay hundreds of millions each year for the kind of Strategy Consulting that I helped to deliver at Deloitte. So it's no surprise that busy individuals with limited resources find formulating and sticking to property investment strategies hard.

Many property investors don't have a clear goal, let alone a strategy. The problem is, without such a plan, it's very easy to take the wrong path, particularly in a fast-changing market. If you don't know where you're going, how do you know how to get there, or if you're getting there? Imagine trying to use Google Maps, without an address or postcode. Of course, it can be done. However, if you use a postcode and mapping tool to find your route in a way that responds to changes in traffic, the journey will be easier and more direct.

Figure 7.1: The right strategy is a clear, efficient path to where you want to be.

In the methodology I've shared, a clear strategy is represented twice. First, at the start, through defining the right Approach. Then at the end, through Adapt, which represents the importance of strategic flexibility.

A well-considered approach will link back to your goals and available resources, as well as the current market context, and it requires you to follow these simple steps:

1. **Start with the end in mind – set clear SMART goals.**
2. **Know your starting point in terms of time, money and industry expertise:**
    - Find out what is needed.
    - Work out what you can bring to the table.
    - Identify the gaps.
3. **Find an efficient, effective and logical path suited to current market circumstances. Make sure it not only fits your goals and starting point, but also takes into account the rewards, relative to the risk, effort and alternatives. This part requires you to:**
    - Acknowledge your start and endpoint.
    - Understand value in the current market context and how to access it.
    - Follow the path: implement.

Adapting to future market changes and trends, if and when required, means you need to:

- Review regularly and when triggered by market or personal change.
- Pause, pivot or persevere.

Having and sticking to a clear, well-thought-through approach and adapting as required can help you to avoid common investor mistakes, such as:

- Making emotional, not strategic decisions.
- Knee jerk decisions – diving in or dithering.
- Relying on trends.

STRATEGY SOUNDBITE CHAPTER SUMMARY

There's a common theme that prevents investors with access to funds from making the most of the opportunities available. Clear, strategically-focused thinking is especially important in today's market.

Firstly, a buoyant market can mask mistakes.

Secondly, as it's harder to find opportunities that work, we fall prey to opportunities that sound too good to be true. For example, you might say you want passive income, and then allocate funds to speculative short-term deals, or you might find fault in opportunities more easily.

Thirdly, as the market has changed, it can't be assumed that factors which drove past trends will continue.

Focusing on value drivers – fundamentals – is more important than ever. A simple three-step approach can be used to design your strategy, or at least begin to think more strategically.

CHAPTER 8

How to start with the end in mind

Investors need a clear strategy: a plan that will take them from their starting point to their end goal. It must take into account their lifestyle considerations and the market.

So how do you create a strategy?

The first and most important component of strategic thinking is knowing what you are aiming for. What's your goal? It might feel like you don't have time to think about what you are aiming for, or that it's obvious: profit! It is very hard to know when you are on track if you don't clarify this upfront. Are you going after yield, capital appreciation or a combined approach based on yield with some form of value appreciation?

In this chapter, I'll outline how a time-tested, simple framework can be used to make this easy and share some tips and ideas to help you to define your goal, and move towards it.

WHAT ARE YOU AIMING FOR?

Surprisingly, few people consider their goals at all, let alone before taking action. Yet the ability to begin with the end in mind is said to be one of the most important factors defining success. Stephen Covey described it comprehensively in his renowned book, *The 7 Habits of Highly Effective People.*[29] Knowing what you are aiming for helps you to maximise your chances of success. Perhaps more importantly for investors seeking to preserve and grow their wealth, it also minimises your chances of failure.

Your big picture goals might include to:

- Make a sustainable, stable profit in a more complex market.
- Leave a legacy for the future; for example, to preserve and grow wealth, build an empire, or a nest-egg for children.
- Have a tangible impact on the world, balancing your social and financial aims.
- Make better returns compared to alternative passive and semi-passive investments.

BEING 'SMART'

The SMART framework was popularised by Peter Drucker in 1954. It stands for Specific, Measurable, Achievable, Realistic and Time-bound.[30] It is a classic, time-tested and effective tool and it is likely that you've come across it before. Tools like this help to take the emotion out of the equation and enable us to see more clearly.

There's plenty of ways to over-complicate property investing and many people do this. My preference is to 'Keep it Simple, Stupid'. The key is not the complexity of the model but how it is applied; for example, in the current market context.

When applied to investing, the SMART framework touches on returns, resources available, risk appetite, and timescales. Returns are the most obvious target in terms of property investment goals. For most investors, they are the whole point. However, potential returns are not the same as actual returns. This is where risk appetite comes in.

When we think about other types of investment, there are generally visible warnings. As the disclaimers say:

> *"The value of your investment can go up or down… past performance does not guarantee future results."*

You won't find such warnings above the front door of the house you're viewing as a potential direct investment. It is, therefore, important to objectively assess risk and your own risk appetite within the scope of your goals. Further, you probably won't be given a guide to the effort required when you look at buying a new property. So, it is also important to understand your own resources and timescales. The SMART framework captures all of this. For example:

Specific

Simone, whose name I have disguised and who I will share more detail about elsewhere in this book, wanted to make an additional net income of £100,000 each year. She wanted to supplement and then replace income from her job so that she could spend more time with her children.

The number and the reason don't matter. What matters is that you are specific and that the specific goal aligns with what you really want. Other investors might focus on earning extra spending money or supporting a retirement plan. If you have more than one important financial goal, you need to prioritise and put the most important goal first.

Measurable

Defining yield or return on investment (ROI) targets and timescales will help you to set your investment criteria. It helps you to confidently find and choose between alternatives. For example, Simone had initially thought she should aim for a higher return, but she simply needed to target a 5% net return on investment each year. Why? Simone was looking for an income of £100,000 per annum. She had been lucky to inherit £2,000,000 so it was a simple case of working back. Other investors might have goals that are 10x higher; the same idea applies. Once you know the target, you can measure opportunities against it.

When it comes to returns, you need to be crystal clear. A simple misunderstanding of definitions can easily equate to hundreds and thousands of pounds. For example, a '5% annual return' might be a 5% gross yield before management costs. This could be hundreds of thousands of pounds a year less than a 5% net return on investment after all costs. This is very important for long-term investors due to the law of compounding returns. For example, let's say Simone is comparing her options:

£2,000,000 @ 5% gross yield might bring in £100,000 gross income. Assuming there is a 30% cost base, this means £70,000 income per year. In five years, Simone would have a paper profit of £381,885.66 assuming compound returns.

The same £2,000,000 @ 5% net income per year would be £100,000 income per year. In five years, that would be a paper profit of £566,717.36.

What if no suitable place was found to invest the money? Inflation continues. She might not actually lose money, but the money she has loses value.

Achievable

It is important to acknowledge what is actually possible to achieve and adjust your targets accordingly.

For example, a well-priced relatively risky development project, subject to planning, might offer a 100% return over three years. That's a return of 33.33% per annum over the investment period. If it goes wrong you could lose your money.

Let's assume this project is priced right for the associated risk. It would then not be achievable to expect a 30-35% return from a passive investment without some kind of risk, such as development risk.

Everyone wants rewards. Unfortunately, it's not possible to sustainably make a huge profit throughout market changes without taking on risk or effort. Anything with potential profit and value is also a question of, and source of, both risk and effort.

Working out what is achievable in the current market, given your risk appetite and what you're able to commit, makes it easier to make well-informed, rational decisions in line with your goals.

This means knowing what types and amounts of risk you are comfortable with. Consider the realities of what others are achieving and how. What is possible and how does your goal compare? I mentioned earlier how many passive or semi-passive investors target 2-6% ongoing, relatively low-risk income per annum. This kind of result is ideal if you are aiming to preserve and grow wealth without putting in a lot of effort or taking on more speculative development risk.

Realistic

Given other competing priorities and preferences, what is realistic for you? A 33% return might be possible if you are happy to be hands-on or have a trusted team to help you. If you have limited time, industry knowledge and contacts then this target might not be realistic. A realistic goal might be to achieve more than you would through available alternatives, such as an existing pension pot. The goal might be to achieve this without sacrificing the time you spend on other important activities.

Time-bound

When will you be ready to invest? Will you invest once, or regularly, and if the latter, how frequently? What's the time horizon for your investments? This will relate back to your goal and starting point. Are you earning well and looking to build a retirement fund? Are you wanting to build an empire or a nest egg for your children or their education? Would you prefer to invest a lump sum then make ongoing contributions to a similar investment pot or platform each month? This is only possible with certain types of investment and will guide what opportunities you look at.

For example, let's say that rather than dithering for three years, which she had at the time we met, Simone had invested £1,000,000 of her inheritance in the first year, into a handful of relatively low-risk opportunities that were forecast to deliver a 5% net income per year from day one. She had originally wanted to achieve a stronger return. However, since she knew she didn't have much time to find anything, she could then have scheduled to invest £100,000 into the handful of selected investments every month until she found an alternative. She would have made more money by investing in lower return projects earlier on than by delaying, missing out on returns and losing out to inflation, and she could always trade out when circumstances or opportunities changed.

Meanwhile, Andrew held off in search of an opportunity with a high potential return. Days, weeks, months and years went by, seemingly in the blink of an eye. When he realised how quickly time was passing, his decision-making became more erratic instead of being time-bound from the outset. He lost additional value for all of the time that he had not invested.

Getting deals done is a numbers game. You can't always predict outcomes, so it is often more useful to set targets and timescales for inputs. For example, will you look at two or 200 opportunities each month? You can use these time-based operational targets and Key Performance Indicators yourself or share them with your team. You can then measure progress against them, and adapt the targets in the future.

WRITING GOALS DOWN

It is worth writing down your goals. This makes it more likely that you'll achieve them. You're more likely to make rational decisions. It's easier to stay on track and respond to changes such as new regulations affecting the market or changes in personal circumstances like a divorce. Compare your written goals with what you have achieved when you're looking at whether you need to pause, pivot or persevere.

The importance of writing goals down was illustrated by a 1979 MBA study on goal-setting.[31] The study supposedly analysed a graduating class to determine how many of them had set goals and a plan for achieving them. The graduating class was asked a single question about their goals in life:

"Have you set written goals and created a plan for their attainment?"

Prior to graduation:

- 84% of the entire class had set no goals at all.
- 13% of the class had set written goals but had no concrete plan.
- 3% of the class had both written goals and concrete plans.

After ten years, the 13% who had written goals, but had not created plans, were making twice as much money as the 84% of the class that had set no goals at all. The 3% that had both written goals and a plan were making ten times as much as the rest of the 97% of the class.

This illustrates the power of setting and writing down goals. On a practical level, things change. So it's also worth reviewing these goals regularly. Set a timescale for review. Annual goal-setting, with quarterly or monthly check-ins, can work well.

TAKEAWAY TIPS

Be laser-focused on what you actually want to achieve.

Be honest with yourself and seek advice from impartial experts about what is achievable in terms of returns, effort and risk in the current market.

Ask yourself and others whether the returns you are targeting are realistic. How do your risk preferences, spare time available, knowledge, contacts and timescales affect the realities of what you can achieve?

Write your SMART goals down and diarise a regular time for reviewing. For example, set goals at the start of a calendar year, and then review them at the start of each month.

STRATEGY SOUNDBITE CHAPTER SUMMARY

If you don't know where you're heading then you won't know when you get there, when you're on track and when you need to tweak your approach.

Setting goals doesn't need to be complicated and it's much easier using a tried and tested framework. Having Specific, Measurable, Achievable, Realistic and Time-bound goals is a great help. Commit to writing them down. Consider sharing your goals with a trusted friend to hold yourself accountable.

Thinking about returns is necessary but not sufficient when defining SMART investment goals. Risks, effort, time and realism are also important.

CHAPTER 9

How to understand your starting point

We've briefly touched on the importance of knowing where you're starting from through the Achievable and Realistic components of the SMART framework. Think of this stage as a simple resource audit. For property investors, it includes a triangle of key resources: money, time and expertise.

WHY IS IT SO IMPORTANT TO KNOW YOUR STARTING POINT?

This part of the methodology is a reality check. We all have limited resources. Trying to do everything yourself in any market environment can be exhausting and it can quickly become another job.

By now it should be clear that ordinary residential property investors are being encouraged to professionalise fast. If you are not able to design your strategy, manage a deal pipeline or run operations properly then you increasingly need to work with someone who can. Understanding what you have and what you need will influence who you work with and how, through business and investment partnerships, professional relationships or joint venture agreements.

On one side of the resource triangle is money: financial resources. On another is time: human resources or effort. The final piece of the puzzle is expertise: intellectual property, skills and local and national market knowledge. For the investors I've worked with, money is not the major constraint. What they need is access to both local and national market knowledge and time.

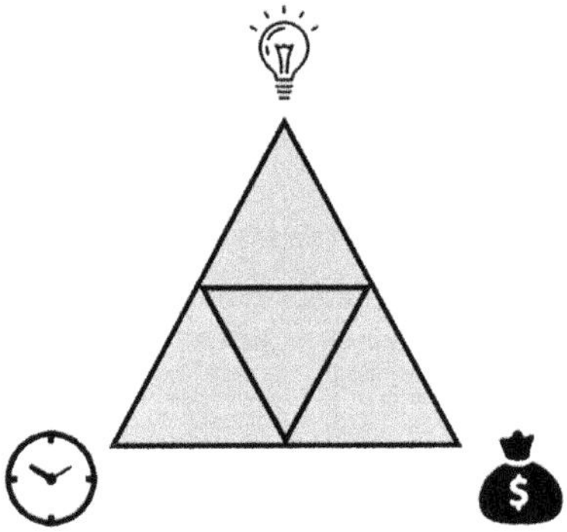

Figure 9.1: You need to have or have access to all three of the key resources in the triangle of money, expertise and time.

With this in mind, you need to:

1. **Find out what is needed.**
2. **Work out what you can bring to the table.**
3. **Identify and fill the gaps.**

Step 1: Find out what is needed across the three essentials of property investment

Working out what money, time, skills, knowledge, local connections, and so on, are needed and then making sure you have what you need requires some knowledge of the activities required and what you are willing and able to do. For example:

Within strategy, you need excellent local and national market knowledge. You also need a strategic lens on your own goals and starting point.

Within deal pipeline management, whether you choose to invest directly or indirectly, you and those you work with will need the skills and ability to:

- Translate strategic goals into clear criteria.
- Access and manage a pipeline of deals.
- Manage transactions and finance set-up for projects.
- Bring together the (sometimes contradictory) advice and compliance requirements of accountants, lenders and lawyers.
- Oversee selection and management of properties carefully, as there are plenty of less scrupulous providers.
- Lead transactions from end-to-end, from site visits to reviewing contracts.
- Deal with new, tougher regulations and finance restrictions.

Within asset management, you can self-manage – which many hugely successful portfolio landlords do, hire a managing agent at a typical cost of 8-12%+ VAT and fees (for example for tenancy renewal), or outsource fully by investing indirectly. Either way, getting these activities right and making sure they are overseen is increasingly important in this more heavily regulated environment. For example:

- Finding and referencing tenants
- Deposit-handling
- Inspections, routine checks, maintenance, gas safety certificates etc.
- Financial reporting
- Dispute management and any emergencies that occur. If a boiler breaks down or there's a break-in, or your tenants damage the property or don't pay their rent, how will this be managed? There are some brilliant apps to help. However, there is no technological replacement for having feet-on-the-ground in some situations.

Asset management requires strong industry and regulatory knowledge and excellent administration. Self-managing properties can be time-consuming, stressful and costly. Even overseeing managing agents is not hassle-free and requires a good understanding of the process. This is especially the case in the set-up phase; for example, making sure the agent is compliant. Later, you may need to respond to unpredictable issues and will want to check that the expected rent is coming in. Ultimately, the buck stops with the investor. Any form of direct investment requires access to the right teams, as well as time, knowledge of process and a professional, trusted team.

Real-life example

Back to Simone. She had £2,000,000 that she wanted to invest in property. She did not have access to a pipeline of profitable deals and, what's more, didn't know of any experienced investor that she trusted enough to partner with. Simone could have achieved so much more if she had sought out someone with the ability to access and assess opportunities, and ultimately secure deals sooner.

Now that you know what is required:

Step 2: Work out what you can bring to the table

It's important to understand what resources you have available. This includes both the financial and non-financial resources of time and expertise. It's also important to know what you have ready access to. Are you starting out with local and national connections in the property sector? Do you have what you need: ready access to deal opportunities and people you have confidence in, and the knowledge to oversee what they're doing?

On money: let's say you have £500,000 in one easily accessible account and access to £2,000,000 from another source that you would like to invest. Perhaps you are in the process of selling a business or family home.

So you have a potential starting investment pot of £2,500,000.

Assuming that the second source of funds is an investment that needs to be liquidated before you can invest, you will have £500,000 now and access to a total of £2,500,000.

No matter what the source of funds is, it makes sense, in my experience, to prepare in advance. You would be making a mistake if you committed to a particular opportunity before the cash hit an easily accessible account. This could easily lead to a waste of effort and money, and you risk the reputational damage of not doing what you say you will.

Some of the investors I've worked with have had access to all the funding they need. Some have had access to a pot of seed capital, and expect to bring on outside investors to make their dreams a reality. Whatever level of financial resources you have, you must understand your starting point. Make sure you have the funding you need before you start to invest.

On time: let's say, you only have two hours a week spare and you would prefer to spend that time with your children or friends, or in the gym. In this case, you have zero hours a week to spend on managing your property investments.

If your goal with investing is to create more time and money to spend with your family, then it may be counter-productive to commit to years of active investing. Make sure you or your team or suppliers have the time required to implement your approach.

On expertise: property is a localised, people-dominated industry, so knowledge, contacts and experience have a strong impact on outcomes. Are you well-versed in local and national market trends, approaches and opportunities or are you a first-time investor? Despite technological advances that have made the sector more accessible and transparent, property is still an industry driven by relationships and people. You will need local and national expertise and contacts in any market. Do you have what you need?

Once you understand which of the resources from the resource triangle you are willing and able to commit, it's time to move on to...

Step 3: Identify and fill the gaps

Identify where the gaps are and what you need someone else to provide. This helps you to make more strategic and less emotional resource allocation decisions.

If you are bringing the money but have little time or knowledge then you will need to get access to people who do have those to offer. This means giving up some control over your investments. If you're investing money then it's important to work with people you can trust.

If you can bring more than one side of the triangle to the table, then you will be able to take more control of your investments if you want to.

For example, let's say you can bring money and another party can bring time and sector expertise in a classic 'sweat equity' joint venture. You could be directly involved and retain control. You would also have to deal with the associated responsibility, accountability and time commitment. Alternatively, you could allocate capital to a property fund. You would have no need to actively oversee this investment and would have less ability to control it.

There's a clear trade-off between resources and control. If you can bring more than one side of the resource triangle then you can take greater control of your investment should you want to. If you are simply bringing the money then it makes sense to favour purely passive investments.

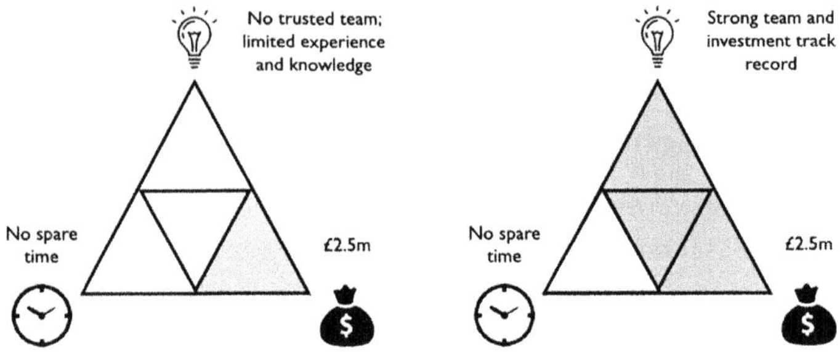

Figure 9.2: If you can bring more than one side of the resource triangle then you can take greater control of your investment should you want to. If you are simply bringing the money and have no spare time or property experience, then you might favour purely passive investments.

As with goals, it helps to go one step further than mentally self-assessing. Write your starting point down. To complete your own resource audit simply fill in the blanks in the following table:

Resource Type	What I need	What I have	The gap and how I will fill the gap
£			
Time			
Expertise			

STRATEGY SOUNDBITE: CHAPTER SUMMARY

In order to grow, you sometimes have to let go. This is even more relevant in a fast-professionalising environment. Take the emotion out of resourcing decisions by honestly assessing what you need and what you can contribute. If you know of a business that can provide a service better, cheaper or faster than you can, then use it. Establish a process for identifying people, teams or products that plug the gaps.

I've mentioned how the idea of sideline investing is becoming less realistic and viable for many investors. Buying a few buy-to-let properties on the side of your job or building a small portfolio is not such an attractive prospect in this fast-professionalising environment. This is largely thanks to the recent tax and regulatory changes covered in earlier chapters.

Are you overwhelmed or bored already by the prospect of interviewing potential providers, requesting external references, and overseeing progress, management and reporting across your portfolio? If so, it makes sense to choose a product suitable for purely passive investment rather than partnering with a joint venture partner or leading the charge yourself.

TAKEAWAY TIPS

Time, money and expertise are required to set your strategy, get deals done and manage investments properly. Once you know what you can bring to the table, it will be clearer whether it is best to invest indirectly or directly.

Make sure you have access to the funding you need before you start to invest and make sure that you or your team have the time and expertise required to implement your approach because you will need local and national expertise and contacts in any market, not least the current environment.

CHAPTER 10

How to design an effective plan that works

The final step required to design a clear strategy for investing is mapping out an efficient, effective and logical pathway which takes into account the market context and your own circumstances. That is the topic of this chapter.

Your approach is a path suited to your aim and your starting point: the resources at your disposal which were discussed in the previous chapter. It must also suit market circumstances and address how you can operate efficiently and effectively within that context. All of this should be thought through before you begin the next stage in your property investment journey.

WHY IS PLANNING YOUR ROUTE SO IMPORTANT?

If you don't acknowledge your own situation and the direction of the market then you may find yourself being dragged along by a strong, unprofitable tide. Refer back to Part 1 if you're not yet clear on the UK residential market context.

The most successful investors see opportunities rather than problems and follow a strategy that works in the circumstances. Their approach is right, and they are able to adapt to suit significant changes, which I will discuss later in the book.

Having an efficient, effective and logical route from your starting point to your goal will result in the greatest long-term success. This means greater rewards, both in absolute terms and relative to alternatives, with less risk and effort.

HOW DO YOU DESIGN AN EFFICIENT, EFFECTIVE AND LOGICAL DIRECTION?

First, you have to understand the resources and requirements that are within your control. Then you must understand the market forces beyond your control. Once you have a direction, all you need to do is implement. This part of the process is simple, in principle.

1. Set the direction: a path from the start to your end goal.

2. Acknowledge market realities and value.

3. Implement.

Digging into these steps:

Step 1: Setting the direction: a path from the start to your end goal

By now, if you've worked through the previous chapters, you should have a set of SMART goals. You should have a good understanding of the resources at your disposal, what you need, and any gaps. You have the starting point for an approach that will move you from your current position to your goal.

If your goals and starting point are simple then your direction can be kept relatively simple too. For most of the investors I've worked with, the reason we have ended up working together is because their situation or requirements are not simple.

Recent examples of the kinds of complexity they face include:

- They have funds but the timing is complicated or contingent on other steps, such as compliance paperwork or international transfers.
- They have seed capital and need to raise more in order to meet their goals, so they need a strategy that works for them and others and they need to consider their capital-raising strategy.
- They have access to funding via a platform so need to put a lot of effort into understanding other investors' requirements.
- They have funds and knowledge but no spare time. They want to retain full control over their investments and have multiple stakeholders from trustees to tax advisors. They need to set a crystal clear plan of action up front and they need a simple reporting mechanism that enables them to keep track of progress and minimise the risk of fraud.

- They have specific and complicated liquidity requirements.
- They face specific tax considerations, so it makes sense to prioritise the use of a specific tax wrapper, such as SIPP, SASS or ISA and this affects whom they can work with.

If your situation is complex or you have an audacious goal and you plan to invest directly, consider working with an impartial strategist who you trust and who does not have a vested interest. There is no right answer. It's not just about applying a cookie-cutter approach to targeting returns, liquidity, risk, timing and so on. There is too much at stake to wing it or follow a readymade strategy on the basis that it has worked for others or in the past.

If you plan to invest indirectly then consider the kind of strategy you want access to. For example, long-term, sustainable income from affordable private rental sector family housing, compared with more speculative prime city centre student housing developments.

Step 2: Recognise market realities and value

Market forces define value and, therefore, the results an investor can expect.

A perfect market is:

> *"...a market in which buyers and sellers have complete information about a particular product and it is easy to compare prices of products because they are the same as each other."*[32]

Undoubtedly, UK property is an imperfect market, and it's easy to see how this is the case. Complete information is impossible to obtain, even for industry professionals. Property values can differ wildly depending on external factors, location, and marketing. Further, property is illiquid: it is time-consuming and challenging to turn assets (for example, houses) into cash.

Anyone who has ever bought or sold a UK property will know how slow and cumbersome the process is, and that's if a seller can find a buyer. As I write, I am recalling the 'For Sale' sign that's been outside my neighbour's property for almost a year. There are plenty of reasons why buying a property is said to be one of the most stressful experiences in our lives.

As a result of such imperfections and imbalances of demand and supply, the market price is not always the same as value. Specialist valuers can be used to gauge the value of properties. Valuations can be subjective. It is an art not a science in most cases due to the many differences between locations and assets. Hot proptech start-ups are working on Artificial Intelligence and complex algorithms to define value as we speak. However, such approaches rely on having enough of the right data and, in an illiquid market, this is often missing. In short, values are not always easy to identify or verify.

In any case, there's also more to understanding Warren Buffet's school of value investing than this. Value investing is about buying well and accessing long-term returns based on fundamentals that won't go out of fashion overnight.

The idea of value investing applies, in principle, just as much to property investment as it does to stocks and shares. In the public markets, decisions made by algorithms are increasingly seen as more efficient and effective. These are preferable to the inherently emotional, slower decisions of humans. There is often insufficient data to replicate this approach in local property markets. The general idea of value investing is still relevant. If you're seeking to preserve and grow wealth, you'll want to focus on undervalued assets that won't go out of fashion and stick with them for the long-term.

Understanding value is crucial for long-term investors and requires a broader appreciation of market forces and fundamentals. Market fundamentals are those factors that define the forces of demand and supply and can be macroeconomic (large-scale) or microeconomic (based on the behaviour of individuals and firms at a more granular scale).

I've outlined key macroeconomic changes in the first part of this book. There is no doubt that this country's massive need for affordable, well-managed accommodation will continue for years to come. As a result, there is still huge value in investing in this kind of UK residential property as an asset.

On a micro level, relevant drivers of fundamental value might include proximity to amenities or transport links. For example, if all other things are equal then a property close to the train station in a commuter town will be worth more than a property further away.

These market forces have fascinated me for many years. I began studying Economics aged 16, began to understand applications in the property market whilst studying at Cambridge, and began to really appreciate the reality when I started investing in regeneration areas of South London, and later, in other regions of the UK.

What I've seen - academically and through practical experience over the years - is that what most is valuable to investors relates to the same three metrics outlined earlier:

- **Risk/reward** – perhaps the most widely discussed ratio in investing. What level of uncertainty is associated with forecast returns?
- **Effort/reward** – what energy and effort are needed to achieve the forecast returns?
- **Opportunity cost** – how does this compare with the alternative options available?

These should be used to define your approach, as well as to define how you adapt.

Worked example

Let's say new regulations make Plan A, investing in a buy-to-let portfolio close to home, more costly and complicated.

However, your Plan B, investing further afield in discounted auction properties, seems too risky and too much effort for the potential reward there is in the current market.

So Plan C, investing the majority of funds with an external service provider or fund becomes the preferred route to follow.

Market-wide regulatory trends are encouraging many to focus on their role as an investor, as being a small- or medium-sized (SME) investor/operator becomes less viable. If your aim is passive investment, it increasingly makes sense to specialise in the role of the financier. If your aim is long-term wealth preservation and creating passive income then it makes sense to focus on long-lasting value.

Thinking strategically like this does not always result in 'sexy' strategies. The good news is it does deliver results over time, thanks to the power of compound returns.

Step 3: Implement

We'll talk in more detail about how to implement your strategy when we move on to deals and operational management. In the words of Jack Welch:

> *"In reality, strategy is actually very straightforward. You pick a general direction and implement like hell."*

STRATEGY SOUNDBITE: CHAPTER SUMMARY

As an investor, you need to take a path that is suited to your aims, resources and the market context. This affects value and how you can access it. Thinking strategically might not feel exciting. However, setting a clear strategy before you invest can save you millions of pounds and even years of anguish.

In the words of Benjamin Franklin:

> *"By failing to prepare, you are preparing to fail."*

Preparing requires you to:

- *Acknowledge your start and endpoint.*
- *Understand value in the current market context.*
- *Implement.*

TAKEAWAY TIPS FOR AVOIDING STRATEGY-LED MISTAKES

For all of the three mistakes linked to strategy, it's important to:

- *Set a clear strategy aligned with your goals, starting point and the market.*
- *Have and follow an action plan that translates the strategy into reality.*
- *Be realistic about rewards, as well as the risk and effort involved and the alternatives to the investment you are looking at.*
- *Work with professionals if you don't have the capacity or expertise to do it all yourself, to define a strategy, access deals and manage them professionally.*

CHAPTER 11

What doesn't work: emotional decisions

In this chapter, I'll share some real-life examples of the kinds of mistakes that investors make when they don't have or follow a clear strategy.

Emotional investment decisions are based on feelings rather than logic, research and fact. For example, if you feel like an opportunity has no downside this may be because you haven't seen the downside yet.

Alternatively, you may feel like you need to make a decision due to a fear of missing out (FOMO). This is likely to be the wrong basis to act on. FOMO is linked to lack of clarity and confidence, and can damage progress and success. Property is emotive and marketers know that. As a result, it can be easy to find yourself going after shiny objects, or following the herd or the heart. A clear strategy helps investors to avoid:

- Highs and lows
- Get-rich-quick schemes
- Unrealistic expectations
- Speculating

These are associated with emotional decision-making. The results can include putting capital at great risk.

WHY IS IT A MISTAKE TO MAKE EMOTIONAL INVESTMENT DECISIONS?

All too often, emotional decisions will give results that are not aligned with what you are aiming for or the realities of the market.

We all get caught up in the heat of the moment. It's human nature to focus on what we are attracted to, even if that doesn't necessarily offer genuine value. However, there is always a cost to making a decision. Choosing one thing means not doing another thing with the same energy or funds. Further, if you try to chop and change then your chances of success are reduced. It sets you back to the beginning each time. It can diminish achievement and the sense of achievement. New shiny objects or opportunities take energy away from more sustainable longer-term opportunities.

It can be easy to lose patience, especially with long-term strategies. However, no grass is greener, except for the grass you water.

Some common examples of heart-over-head property investment choices include:

- **Development opportunities.** These are not a good choice if the investment goal is wealth preservation or preparing for retirement.

- **Falling in love with a property.** Investors don't tend to fall in love with stocks and shares. In fact, this would be frowned on. However, property investment has taken on an emotional dimension, which can encourage investors to make decisions led by the heart.

- **Buying property you want or could use or rent out.** It's tempting to have choices. You could use that pied à terre in town in the week, maybe with a bit of Airbnb at the weekends, or rent it out longer term if circumstances change. There is always a trade-off. Could funds have earned better returns elsewhere, and those greater returns be used to fund your lifestyle decisions?

- **Not seeing the downside.** For example, you're offered a 'guaranteed rent' for a period of time and assume the best, rather than asking questions. Don't be afraid to be cynical: such incentive schemes are generally in place for marketing purposes, often because the properties wouldn't sell without them. The guaranteed rent may be much higher than the market rent. Be afraid, whenever something looks too good to be true.

- **Chasing yield.** If you want to create extra income, it's natural to go after higher yields. High gross yields or potential returns come at a cost in terms of the area, building or tenant quality. If you want to preserve wealth to pass on to future generations, for example, then you will need to pick high quality assets in areas that have strong and growing demand relative to supply. This generally means accepting a lower headline yield than you would achieve in an area with low growth prospects, an outdated building or a property with a higher risk tenant type.

Real-life example: emotional decision-making

An investor I've known for many years fell into this trap. Like so many of the investors I work with, Ben – not his real name – is very busy, and highly intelligent. He's a Partner at a leading London law firm. He wanted to buy some hassle-free properties for his children, who were at university. The goal was to provide them with a fall-back option: if it all went wrong, he thought, they'd always have the income.

A colleague mentioned that she was investing in a stunning new build development in Oxford, which he had loved since his university days. He did not want to miss out. Ben spoke to the sales agent and looked over the brochure. It showed a stunning, hassle-free opportunity that he could happily live in. The Computer Generated Images (CGIs) were seductive. The opportunity promised a 'guaranteed 6% return' for two years. He also got a sense of security from knowing that a building warranty was in place. There was only a handful left. He was able to negotiate a discount for buying more than one property, off-plan.

Ben bought six apartments for £2,000,000.

The first mistake Ben made was being driven by a fear of missing out. He felt that if his colleague could do it, so could he. The second mistake was believing it would be best to invest in properties he could envisage himself living in. The third mistake was relying on marketing materials and incentives like the guaranteed rent, discount, building guarantee, and stunning CGI images. In his eyes, these had made the opportunity seem both perfect and easy, which was exactly what he wanted.

Looking back, Ben realised he should have done more research.

We calculated the difference between what he made for his children net of all the costs. We compared this with what they might have earned elsewhere. When he recognised the difference in results, he realised they were earning less than 100% of what they might have done. They lost out on hundreds of thousands of pounds over the course of the investment.

Since then, he's begun to build a substantial portfolio for his children, strategically. He targets maximum net income over the long-term through indirect investments. The portfolio is designed to deliver exactly what he wanted: a safety net for his children so that they will never need to worry in a way that minimises the involvement required by him and ultimately his children.

TAKEAWAY TIPS

- *If you feel emotional about an investment opportunity, your biggest priority is to take a step back.*
- *Watch out for the fear of missing out or feeling competitive when friends or colleagues mention an opportunity.*
- *Don't let yourself fall in love with an idea or image, this is a clear sign of emotional rather than strategic decision-making.*
- *Make sure you have a clear strategy before you invest.*
- *Make sure that your strategy is an efficient, realistic way to move towards your goals, addressing your priorities, starting point and the market.*
- *Make sure you do thorough research on each opportunity and look for the downside as well as the upsides.*
- *Remember that if something looks too good to be true, it probably is.*

CHAPTER 12

What doesn't work: diving in or dithering

In this chapter, I'll give examples of what can happen if you dive into property investing or dither around the edges. In an age of distraction and busy-ness we're all time-poor. It can easily feel like there isn't enough time to do a lot of research.

Some people respond to overwhelm by diving in. You might have scratched the surface with research but not yet built up enough knowledge to make the best investment decision. Snap decisions can easily result in lacklustre returns or even losing money.

The flip side to diving in is dithering. Through fear, ditherers will over-analyse and delay. This is becoming easier in our digital environment: you can research endlessly with the help of the internet. It's becoming even easier to find fault with every opportunity. This creates plenty of excuses not to invest. Dithering can result in leaving capital sitting around, making low, no or negative real returns for far longer than is necessary. Not investing is one of the most certain ways an investor can ensure that they don't make a strong return.

WHY IS THIS A MISTAKE?

Best practice in making investment decisions involves having a financial target. The two extreme approaches of diving in recklessly or being paralysed by dithering ignore the need to focus on a clear goal. Both approaches result in poor allocations of the investor's most precious resources: time, effort and capital.

Real-life example: dithering

Simone, who I mentioned earlier, was fortunate enough to inherit £2,000,000. She was keen to invest and initially attended many local property events to research her options. Three years later, around the time we met, she had still not actually made an investment. Nerves or excuses had got the better of her every time she came close to buying. Like Goldilocks' porridge, nothing was 'just right'. It was only when we began to discuss her situation that Simone discovered that, over the course of those three years, her £2,000,000 inheritance had lost at least £270,000 in real value, just to keep pace with modest inflation. That's when things changed, and she set a more achievable target of 5% return on investment, which enabled her to meet her goal, and which she duly achieved.

Real-life example: diving in

On the flip side, Andrew worked at a large global bank. His hours were punishing. He was keen to invest ASAP to create an income that would allow him to step out of the rat race. He received a tip-off about an affordable 'below market value' block of flats in Liverpool going to auction. The auction sales brochure described working tenants and listed the rent coming in from Day One (known as passing rent) as £150,000 per annum. Each flat was priced so low that he thought: 'How can I lose money?' All of his friends at the bank had done the 'northern buy-to-let thing'. The yield seemed so good compared with London, and the pricing was cheap. The mistake he made was diving straight in when he had no trusted teams on the ground and no local knowledge.

Simone and Andrew ended up losing out by a similar amount in terms of time wasted, money lost and extra stress, which could all have been avoided.

Property investment requires three things: time, expertise and money.

For investors like Simone and Andrew, who have money but no specific sector expertise, it's important to work with people who do. Today, both are investing in genuinely passive investments: indirect funds that mean they get access to the UK residential property market without the hassle that is so often associated with directly working on transactions and management.

Remember that knee-jerk decisions are rarely the best decisions when it comes to investing. To avoid them, you need to translate your strategy into an action plan with clear targets and then follow the plan. Get as specific as you can. For example, set a goal around how many opportunities you'll look at. Professional funds often discount between 90-99% of opportunities. If you want to invest directly then having a strong pipeline and clear, realistic targets is a great way to avoid diving in or dithering. You can make more objective, strategic decisions to invest or walk away when you are not worried about having access to other opportunities and you'll quickly learn what works and what doesn't.

If you have no spare time, then investing will likely involve working with specialists in the field. As market and regulatory pressures have increased, it's increasingly important for investors like Simone and Andrew, without local and national sector expertise, spare time or teams on the ground, to work with people who do have the time and expertise needed.

TAKEAWAY TIPS

Make sure you have measurable objectives and a timeline for when you will invest. If you are bored by the prospect of establishing a process for managing a great deal pipeline or see it as a poor use of your time, then it may make more sense to choose a product that is suitable for purely passive investment rather than leading the charge yourself. Once you take into account the cost of your time, it is often both easier and more efficient.

I've said it before, and it's worth repeating: if it sounds too good to be true, it probably is.

Make sure you research your options thoroughly and remember there is no perfect option. Don't just think about goals: be clear on your priorities as there is always a trade-off and no decision is still a decision.

Mitigate your risks up front. Manage nerves and risks by focusing on liquidity (how quickly can you access your funds?) and diversification (are your risks spread out so that a bad apple doesn't wipe you out?).

Take the emotion out of decision-making for specific opportunities. Honestly assess what you need and what you have. Establish a process for identifying people, teams or products that plug any gaps. In this new regulatory environment, the idea of sideline investing is becoming less viable. Acquiring a few buy-to-let properties on the side of your job is not such an attractive prospect in this fast-professionalising market. This is largely thanks to the recent tax changes (such as Section 24), and the increased cost and complexity of complying with regulations in favour of tenant rights (from licensing to the Tenant Fees Act 2019) and in favour of improved environmental performance of buildings (for example via Minimum Energy Efficiency Standards).

CHAPTER 13

What doesn't work: relying on trends

Trends create headlines. The trouble is that extrapolating from headlines can oversimplify matters. This can result in multi-million-pound losses for investors.

For example, contrary to what some capital-dwellers believe, there is a whole country out there beyond London. It can be easy to think that the London property market reflects what's going on in the rest of the country. That's simply not the case. Even within London, there are so many micro-markets. One part of London can be underpinned by very different drivers compared to another part.

Then there's the tendency to look at past performance and expect that future performance in an area will be the same. It can be easy to believe the mantra of capital growth, regardless of affordability constraints or regulatory changes. Don't assume property will always grow in value or past price rise trends will continue just because they always have so far. Allocating capital based on past rather than current market drivers can lead to over- or under-investing in specific niches or geographies.

WHY IS THIS A MISTAKE?

Whilst you won't see a risk disclaimer above the door of a terraced house, past performance in the property market is not an indicator of future success. Micro area knowledge is crucial in an imperfect market where the performance of an asset can differ, based on which end of a street it's located. Don't assume a property's future performance will mirror historic area trends or other people's predictions.

Real-life example: relying on trends

Natasha and her sister had access to £5,000,000 from their father as an early inheritance. They loved Clapham, an attractive part of London. Period properties in the capital had delivered strong returns for their parents and friends. So they thought this approach would be a winner. Surely, the area would continue to go up in value.

They invested in a small portfolio of charming Victorian properties. The plan was to live in two of them and rent the others until they both settled down and then sell for a profit. They did not understand that London trends don't apply to every property in every area and market. London contains so many markets, and new drivers are creating new trends and micro trends within the city.

They did not understand that past performance does not predict future success. And they did not realise that the estate agent predicting area growth had not taken account of affordability issues or political uncertainties. How many people would be willing and able to buy the properties they had acquired at a price higher than they had paid?

The biggest mistake they made was assuming that price rises would continue based on historical trends and anecdotal evidence. They had bought at a market peak and soon realised how few people wanting to live in Clapham could afford to buy at the prices they would need to sell for in order to make a profit. What had worked for their parents and friends for ten to twenty years seemed unlikely to work in the near future. They realised they had made a mistake.

When Natasha came to invest again, this time with her fiancé, she looked at strategy first. They took a very different approach. What they really wanted was a way to preserve and grow their wealth for their future children.

Initially, they had resisted investing far from home in unknown territory or giving up control. Once they understood the fundamentals affecting the market, they changed their approach. No longer would the mantra of capital growth guide their decisions. No longer did they believe that keeping control would result in safer and more profitable outcomes. They invested further afield, and they invested via a fund. Their real goal was income generation and wealth preservation rather than capital growth. Their portfolio has been delivering a reliable, regular income and its value has increased since then, though they weren't relying on this to make a return.

TAKEAWAY TIPS

- *Remember that a buoyant market can mask mistakes and may not last. Factors that drove past trends can't be assumed to continue. If the opportunity works without assuming capital growth, then it works. Be clear on where your profits are coming from. If you are relying on growth then you are leaving your returns to forces beyond your control, with all the risk that this entails.*

- *Regardless of the quality of any single property you invest in, in a fast-moving context with new tax and regulatory changes to navigate, the strategies that worked well a few years ago are unlikely to work so well now.*

- *In times of uncertainty, it might be tempting to invest in areas or strategies that you know have worked historically. However, some of those opportunities may well be already past their best. Focusing on value drivers – the fundamentals that drive demand and supply – is more important than ever.*

- *Think carefully about the source of insights you are planning to base decisions on. Work with specialists who can share insights into what's really driving the market The Political, Economic, Social, Technological, Legal and Environmental (PESTLE) considerations and changes described elsewhere in this book are a great starting point.*

- *Don't rely on assumptions based on the past or what you have learned online or from friends. If you have read about it in the newspaper or heard advice from a taxi driver, that insight may well be already past its best.*

- *Assume there is no perfect investment. Seek advice from multiple sources and at least one unbiased professional who has nothing to sell. One easy way to research a specific opportunity is to triangulate. This means using more than one method to collect data on the same topic. This helps you to validate and capture different dimensions of the same thing. For example, research the facts online beyond what you find on property websites or in newspapers. Speak to an impartial specialist. If it's a direct investment then call around three to five local estate agents to get their perspectives on price, value and the direction of the market. Don't be afraid to get an objective perspective by pretending to be a buyer, seller or valuer. Test any comparable evidence you are given. For example, just because a property is being marketed at £1,000,000, this doesn't mean it will sell at that level. Look at the time it takes to sell and actual sold prices, as well as qualitative factors.*

STRATEGY SOUNDBITE CHAPTER SUMMARY

For all of the three mistakes mentioned, there's a common theme that prevents investors with access to funds from making the most of the opportunities available: the lack of clear strategic thinking. This is especially important in today's complex market.

Firstly, it is harder to mask mistakes.

Secondly, it is harder to find opportunities that genuinely work. This can make you more likely to fall prey to opportunities that seem too good to be true or to reject opportunities that seem faulty when they are not.

Thirdly, as the market has changed, factors that drove past trends should not be assumed to continue. Focusing on value drivers – fundamentals – is more important than ever.

SECTION 3

Deals

CHAPTER 14

How to access and assess the opportunities that are right for you

Once you've designed your path, or at least have an idea of how to get one, you need to implement the plan of action. To do so, and whether you choose to invest directly or indirectly, you need to access and assess deals. This relies on setting the deal criteria aligned with your strategy, managing a strong pipeline and ensuring quality transactions.

That is the topic of this chapter.

Strategy and deal criteria are closely connected. Strategy defines and reflects the performance, ease and risk associated with the deals you do. It influences your criteria, which, in turn, influences your pipeline and transactions. To put it bluntly, if the idea of managing a deal pipeline and transactions puts you off or feels like more effort than it's worth then investing directly may not be the right route for you to take.

In the methodology I've outlined, two steps represent the right deal criteria and quality transactions:

- **Assess** – this step is about defining your criteria and assessing individual opportunities against them.
- **Access** – this step is about knowing how and where to find the right opportunities.

ASSESS

Assessing deals successfully requires the 6 Ds. You need to:

- Set the right Deal Criteria (D1).
- Include Due Diligence (D2) and Diversity (D3): know your numbers and balance your risks.
- Adopt a clear approach to Decision-making (D4), Delivery Capabilities (D5) and Delegation (D6) – choose between DIY, DWY, or DFY.

ACCESS

Within accessing deals, there are three simple steps:

Step 1: Manage a strong pipeline of opportunities, meaning you have enough potential deals to choose from,

Step 2: Have the ability to filter down, and

Step 3: Have the capability to manage quality transactions.

On steps 1 and 2, your deal pipeline is characterised by:

- Number of deals
- Average deal size
- Percentage of completed deals
- Average time to completion.

This is a numbers game. It's important to have enough of the right kind of opportunity to select from. For example, you might assume that if you're investing directly, you will have to offer on at least ten deals to get one agreed that offers a decent return, that each deal will take 12 weeks to complete and that one third of deals will fall through, which is the industry average in residential property. You can then work out how many deals you need to review and offer on, in order to do the number of deals you want to. Make sure the operator you're investing with has a strong pipeline like this and the ability to sift through to select the most suitable options, if you're investing indirectly.

On step 3, you need the ability to manage quality transactions. Plenty of deals fall through even after they have been agreed, especially in the English property market. Poor communication, weak acceleration and lazy processing, as well as factors beyond your control, can derail a transaction.

These steps require you to decide the extent of your involvement. Would you prefer a DIY, DWY or DFY product or service?

All of this is important because successfully assessing and accessing deals helps investors to avoid common expensive mistakes. These include mistaking price for value, misunderstanding timing, and speculating.

STRATEGY SOUNDBITE: CHAPTER SUMMARY

Deal criteria are connected to strategy. To successfully assess and access deals, you or the people you work with need to cover off some key activities. You need to know your criteria. You need to make accurate assessments. You need a strong pipeline of opportunities. You need the resources and team to complete transactions.

The ability to assess and access suitable deals helps investors to avoid wasting time, effort and money. A good approach to assessing and accessing deals helps investors to avoid common expensive mistakes. These include mistaking price for value, misunderstanding timing, and speculating.

CHAPTER 15

How to assess deals with limited information and resources

This chapter highlights what you need to know in order to assess deals when you have limited information and resources. Assessing deals can be time-consuming. It requires a clear approach as well as some mathematical and local expertise. You will need the 6Ds:

- The right Deal Criteria (D1) – this is about knowing what you're looking for and making sure it is in line with your approach.
- Diversity (D2) and comprehensive Due Diligence (D3) – this is about knowing your numbers and minimising risks.

- Delivery Capabilities, Delegation and Decision-making (D4, D5 and D6) – these are about making the most of the resources you have and making sure you have what you need by working with the right teams in the right ways.

D1: THE RIGHT DEAL CRITERIA

Having clear deal criteria means that you know what you want as an investor. It helps you to know if an opportunity is right for you and will help move you further from or closer to your goal. You need to ensure that your investments fit with your strategy and its components: your goal, starting point and the market context.

Deal criteria are requirements around risk, resources, effort and target returns. These can be translated into characteristics, such as tenure, tenant type, and location features, for direct investments. Having this laid out clearly enables you to make decisions and prioritise opportunities efficiently and effectively.

Whether it's a passive income of 3% per annum or a riskier approach targeting 6% per annum, having clear targets and criteria makes assessing deals easier. You can quickly identify and capitalise on those opportunities that fit and easily discount all others.

Examples of goal-driven criteria metrics used frequently to compare opportunities against targets, and to compare with one another include:

YIELD

This is your earnings, expressed as a percentage of the asset's market value or face value. Popular measures include the following:

- Gross yield, which is gross asset income divided by market value.

- Net yield, which is net asset income (after operating expenses, for example: management, maintenance, voids etc) divided by market value. This measure includes one-off expenses, such as Stamp Duty Land Tax. Be aware: some providers will make assumptions for you. They might assume specific finance costs, forecast capital growth and maintenance costs. Relevant costs may be excluded or minimised for the purposes of marketing literature. Not everyone is incentivised to be honest about the numbers. Agents you speak to may not have full knowledge. If you are making investment decisions then do your own calculations on the basis of your own assumptions. This requires some level of market insight as well as objectivity.

NET INCOME

- For properties, net income is rent less management, maintenance, voids etc. Be sure to compare like with like and understand the calculations.

- For property shares, net income is income after all costs, including management fees.

ONGOING RETURN ON INVESTMENT FOR LONGER-TERM PROJECTS

- For properties, this is net rental return per annum divided by equity invested.

- For shares, this is net income per annum divided by shareholders' equity.

RETURN ON INVESTMENT FOR SHORT-TERM 'VALUE ADD' PROJECTS

- Return on investment (ROI) is the difference between the current value of the investment and the cost of that investment, divided by the cost of the investment.

INTERNAL RATE OF RETURN

- The rate at which Net Present Value is 0. This measures how well the investment performs over time. Closely related is your target turnaround time to positive return, whether selling or renting.

DEAL SIZE

- This will affect capital required, your pace of growth, focus and ability to diversify and specialise.

Worked example: comparing long term rental properties

Let's say, you're looking to invest in some buy-to-let property. One option is a portfolio of terraced houses, priced at £800,000 and the current rent to working tenants is £8,000 per month.

(£8,000x12)/£800,000 = 12% gross yield.

If it aligns with the market average, you can expect 30% costs. Some sources will tell you your cost assumption should be lower; however, this is a relatively safe and realistic assumption, once you account for maintenance, management and voids. It is what banks typically assume. So you're looking at a net income of £67,200, an 8.4% net yield assuming no finance.

Then there's a block of new build flats priced at £1,200,000 in the city centre. It offers a forecast rent of £9,500 per month.

£9,500x12 = £114,000 = 9.5% gross yield.

A novice investor might prefer the new build option, which offers a higher forecast return in total. However, for new builds, the forecast rent often exceeds the market rents in the area. This option also ignores important costs. Sure, you won't have to spend anything to get it ready to let. However, there's no escaping ongoing management, compliance, maintenance costs and voids. These relate as much to tenants as to the age of the building over a long term time horizon.

So, knowing what you do about the costs, would you choose the terraced houses or the new build flats?

Look at it this way:

	Property A Existing	Property B New Build
Property purchase price	£800,000	£1,200,000
Current rent per month	£8,000	£9,500
Gross rent per annum	£96,000 (proven)	£114,000 (forecast)
Gross yield	12%	9.50%
Typical costs (~30%)	£28,800	£34,200
Net income per annum	£67,200	£79,800
Net yield	8.40%	6.65%

Figure 15.1 Comparison of property purchase price, rental incomes, gross and net yields to make more logical decisions.

Understanding the numbers and how to interpret them is key. Being bad with numbers or not being able to use a spreadsheet is a good indicator that you should either get better or let someone else take care of this. If the idea of assessing deals brings you out in a rash, focus on a less direct approach and minimise your involvement in assessing deals, unless your criteria are so easy to meet that they will be met by most properties on the market.

Even the smartest investors run into difficulties when they need to decide between alternatives in property. This is a key factor in people not taking action. They are overwhelmed by choice. You will be unsurprised that I suggest going back to your goals to create criteria that align with your priorities. When you have that information you'll be in a much better position to understand which deals make sense for you.

TAKEAWAY TIPS

- *Set criteria aligned with your approach. Don't be side-tracked by other people's criteria, or opportunities that don't match your criteria.*
- *Take into account returns and also risk, effort and alternatives.*
- *Measure opportunities against your criteria.*
- *When you compare opportunities with each other, or with your criteria, be sure to compare like with like.*

Now let's look at diversity and due diligence. This is about knowing the returns, costs and chances, taking everything into account and spreading your risk.

D2: DIVERSITY

D2, Diversity, means making sure you have a mix, so you don't end up 'overweight' in a particular approach or area.

Risk is important as it has the capacity to make or break a deal. Diversity is a great way to reduce portfolio risk.

Example

Let's say, you want to invest £1,000,000 this year. It might seem like the easiest and most sensible approach is to put all of your money into a single deal. What happens if that deal goes wrong and ends up losing 20% of its value? You lose £200,000.

Alternatively, you might invest £200,000 each across five smaller investments. Even if one of these investments loses its full value, and the others deliver modest returns, you will still be better off.

Let's say four of the investments make a modest return averaging 3%. One loses 100% of its value. You will still be better off than in the undiversified scenario, losing £176,000, as you won't have all your eggs in one basket.

D3: DUE DILIGENCE

Once you have the right criteria and an idea of how much you want to spread your risks, you need the ability to make accurate assessments. D3, Due Diligence, is about understanding and considering costs and returns objectively and accurately. Be thorough with your research. Understand the market. This will enable you to make better investment decisions.

It's important to ensure that you are always comparing like with like, and you understand what is going into the calculations. This is because what one sales agent or investment business describes as yield or return may exclude relevant and important costs. Assumptions can also vary wildly. For example, I've received plenty of deals that state they offer a '10% return'. However, when I dug into the numbers, substituting realistic costs for hopeful costs, they offered less than half of what was promised. Rents might be inflated. Management and maintenance costs might be underestimated. Finance and transaction costs might be ignored, and so on.

Researching local markets is important as different locations can differ wildly. Understand values and keep it simple. Investing directly in property is not like the stock market, where data is more public, fast-moving and analysed at all hours of the day by experts in the field. Information is less easily available in the real-world property market. You can use online and information tools like Zoopla and Rightmove to do desktop research into a local area. There's plenty of free and relatively low-cost data services and these can be invaluable for investors looking to get to know new parts of the market. However, the market for real assets is significantly slower than the market for stocks.

It's key to understand the economics and fundamentals of an opportunity, like existing and future demand and supply. Know the factors affecting areas. Examples include proximity to fundamentals, such as transport, workplaces, amenities and educational establishments.

You will also need to have a good idea about who lives in the area. How old are they? Where do they work and what do they do? Do they have children? Where are the leisure amenities they use?

You must research strategies, locations and specific opportunities fully. Then investigate the teams and businesses that you are considering investing with in order to work out if they are the right team for you, based on their track record and reputation.

If you invest with a platform or investment business, you won't be able to review every decision. In this situation, familiarise yourself with their priorities. For example, how do they identify the right areas? What does a fundamentals search reveal about their past choices? Do they focus on transport/connectivity, amenities and jobs? How about regeneration and inward investment? What size of assets do they focus on?

Finally, you will need to think about when to invest. Does your research suggest you should invest now, or wait a while? Make sure your due diligence includes checking that timing is in line with your long-term goals, whether you have decided to be a hands-on or hands-off property investor.

Recognise that your criteria should not be solely based on returns. You must consider your attitude towards risk, available time and alternatives.

TAKEAWAY TIPS

- *Do thorough due diligence on each opportunity.*
- *Identify and research factors affecting opportunities, including local values and market trends. It can be useful to use the PESTLE (Political, Economic, Social, Technological, Legal, Environmental) framework on a micro level to do this.*
- *Use diversity to protect yourself against the downsides of specific opportunities. Whether you are self-managing or investing via a fund, it makes sense not to have all of your eggs in one basket. Make sure you are not over-dependent on specific value drivers, such as a single employer or regulation.*

D4, D5 AND D6: DECISION-MAKING, DELEGATION AND DELIVERY CAPABILITIES

Now let's move onto making the right decisions, objectively and dispassionately. For this, you need to make decisions in line with your criteria and an objective assessment of the numbers. D4 is Decision-making, D5 is Delegation and D6 is Delivery Capabilities. When it comes to assessing opportunities, you can:

- Do the work yourself (DIY)
- Seek some professional support (DWY) or
- Get someone to do the work for you (DFY) and invest indirectly.

You can use your own decision-making framework and analytical capabilities. Or you can delegate to others. What if analysing and deciding on a large volume of opportunities feels like too much work? Delegate to others with a strong pipeline and delivery capabilities.

Either way, you need a clear understanding of costs and risks, and a clear way to decide what is suitable. For every deal that works, 90-99% may not. You need to analyse and filter those deals, and this demands in-depth local knowledge.

Even in a digital age, where so much is available online, there is an asymmetry of information. There can be significant differences between streets right next to one another: "Oh, you meant north of the bridge on Station Road, not south? No, that area has a completely different feel, and you'll never get that kind of premium there." It takes time and effort to gain the specific local knowledge required. It helps to have people you can bounce ideas off who have their incentives aligned with yours. You need to cultivate and nurture relationships to get the information you need. For example, for London-based investors investing further afield, you will need someone you trust to differentiate between what price level is local, and what is seen by locals as a 'London price' and, therefore, what decision to make.

Estate agents and developers often have good local knowledge. However, they are incentivised to maximise their fee rather than your returns. Investors often don't have the local knowledge they need and are incentivised to minimise costs and maximise returns.

Both parties are dependent on one another, even though it's clear their incentives are not aligned. Worse still, the search process often requires the investor to share proof of funds early on, meaning they often end up declaring their ability to pay. Clever negotiation tactics abound and can easily mislead investors. Sweeteners such as 'guaranteed returns' are positioned as being to the investor's advantage. These are often marketing ploys. There are plenty of stories of agents fabricating competition to encourage quicker sales at higher prices.

TAKEAWAY TIPS

- *Have a clear framework for making decisions, or work with someone who has. You need to be able to identify and discount opportunities that don't stack up. If you're investing directly, this could be 99% of the opportunities in your pipeline. You must 'go for no', as the sales manuals say.*
- *Investors also need to have some industry knowledge and experience in order to access plenty of deals and then be able to filter down to the best.*
- *When you receive or request information, always consider the motives of its source. 'Triangulate' by seeking independent sources to verify and provide their input. Ideally, you want 3+ opinions to match up.*

STRATEGY SOUNDBITE: CHAPTER SUMMARY

When you have limited time, information and resources, you need a clear, suitable process to assess opportunities efficiently and effectively. You need clear deal criteria suited to your strategy: defined by your starting point and goal. You need to understand the metrics used most often by investors to compare opportunities against targets and one another. Comprehensive due diligence and diversity are needed. Then you need to consider decision-making processes, pipeline delivery capabilities and delegation so that you can invest successfully despite inevitably limited resources.

CHAPTER 16

How to access the right opportunities

Access to resources and opportunities is key for investing: if you can't access it, you can't invest in it. A key problem that potential investors face is the lack of easy access to suitable opportunities, which we'll turn to now.

What access means on a practical level is having a good volume of opportunities to choose from, and the ability to carry out quality transactions.

STEP 1: HAVE ACCESS TO A STRONG PIPELINE OF OPPORTUNITIES AND STEP 2: HAVE THE ABILITY TO FILTER DOWN

What potential investors need will depend on their approach. In my experience, any form of direct investment requires access to a strong deal pipeline: a funnel of opportunities to filter down and select from. It requires the resources and ability to sift leads down and negotiate. Incidentally, the same is required for home buyers.

The average first-time buyer will view eight properties before they agree on a property to buy. The percentage of properties an investment buyer will review and discount can be as high as 99%. To review a high volume of opportunities and sort the wheat from the chaff you need a good process around assessing deals. Indirect investment approaches require you to have access online or via intermediaries to the same capabilities.

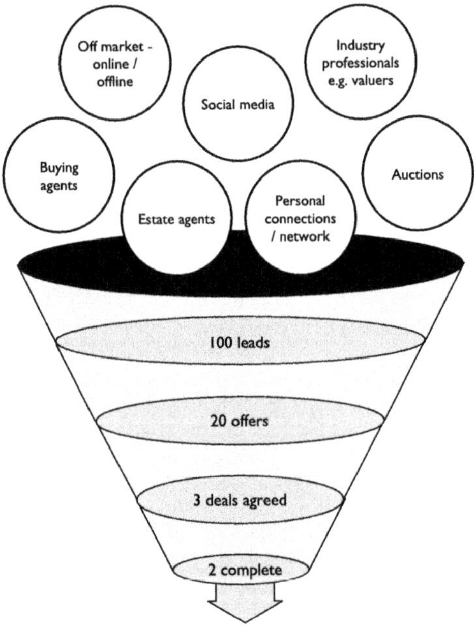

Figure 16.1: Accessing the right deals is a numbers game. You need access to a larger number of opportunities, ideally from multiple sources, and the ability to filter down.

The reality for private investors is that we live in an age of busy-ness. Staying on top of existing personal and professional commitments and a deal pipeline can feel unrealistic. Then there is the obvious geographical restriction in property. This is especially problematic for sideline investors who already have a demanding career and have strictly limited time to commit. For example, if you want to focus on investments with a good yield in the UK, then the North of England might be a great place to find deals. However, if you're not based in that market and planning on investing directly, then you need local knowledge, connections and the ability to travel regularly to those areas.

Resolving this issue links back to what resources you have available. Investors need to think about how much control they want to have. They must consider their personal circumstances, and what stage they are at in their life. They must acknowledge the market environment. These factors will influence the choices they make.

For many time-poor investors, the priority is leveraging others. Going solo in a professionalising market is unrealistic. As a result, the question is less whether you should work with others, and more, how to do so, and who with.

Michael Porter noted that strategy is about making choices and trade-offs. This applies to how a financial return goal translates into the realities of investing and doing deals. It requires criteria and trade-offs.

The next and final step in accessing deals is:

STEP 3: HAVE THE CAPABILITY TO MANAGE QUALITY TRANSACTIONS

Direct investments require a strong team to manage conveyancing, acceleration and administration. For indirect opportunities, this is more about timing; for example, do you want to invest a lump sum or invest over time through 'pound cost averaging'. Again, consider D4 and D5, Delegation and Delivery Capabilities.

DO IT YOURSELF, DONE WITH YOU OR DONE FOR YOU?

One of the biggest decisions investors need to make is on what basis do they want to invest. This should be based on their goals, circumstances and the market context. Investors need to decide if they want to invest solo, Do It Yourself (DIY).

They might also work with a Done With You (DWY) operator if they are keen to be involved and have some spare time.

Finally, they might choose a Done For You (DFY) approach, which is the most commonly used among the investors I've worked with. These options apply to the Access, Assess and Asset Management components of the methodology.

To help you decide between DIY, DWY and DFY, I'll share a little more about what each of these means below in relation to access:

Do It Yourself

To more comprehensively cover the Do it Yourself approach to finding deals would take another book. It is also a time-consuming and energy-intensive process for potential investors. In relation to accessing deals specifically, DIY includes:

- Building relationships in your target locations
- Assessing and filtering countless opportunities, and
- Having presence and insight 'on the ground' to avoid missing out on opportunities.

Done With You

A Done With You approach still requires you to have some time and an understanding of the market. DWY offerings generally enable you to retain decision-making control and responsibility. This can be a good thing if you know the market well and have time to contribute. For example, the provider identifies an opportunity and you buy it. They might develop, manage and/or sell it, taking their cut at each stage of the way.

You are dependent on your service provider and their level of skill. Dare I say it, some DWY service providers have a reputation for being less than scrupulous. This includes some providers with a strong and positive online profile. Plenty of investors have been burned in this way because there's not much regulation in this part of the sector. That is why it's still important to know your stuff, even if you're not leading every activity. You need to ensure that deals stack up and your service provider is knowledgeable, legal and ethical.

In relation to access, DWY might involve a property sourcing business with local access to opportunities in a regional market. The plan might be for you to build your own portfolio. The service provider identifies the potential assets, and you decide and acquire the property. Getting access to deals through a DWY service can work. It's best if incentives are structured right. Good oversight is needed. In short, the problem of information asymmetry in the market in accessing deals is not overcome by working with a local provider.

Done For You

This is a wholly hands-off approach to property investment. There are more 'Done For You' options available now. Property has become more specialised due to market changes. The roles of investor and manager are increasingly separated.

DFY gives investors easier access. Often, not just to one deal but to a whole portfolio. For example, the provider might be via:

- A listed property business, such as a Real Estate Investment Trust (REIT). These are often specialised in a specific sector (for example, student housing), and diversified across multiple assets.

- An alternative finance platform, such as an equity crowdfunding platform, or peer to peer lending platform. You may be able to pick your own investments and receive a passive return, and you are in control of allocating funds to diversify.

- Via a broader institutional investment vehicle, such as a pension fund. The institution might own significant real estate holdings. Whilst the returns are typically relatively low, they are, in principle, lower risk due to diversification. This does not necessarily mean that the risk/reward ratio is better. Investors discovered this in recent market crashes. In general, however, your financial advisor is more likely to recommend working with a large institutional investor than they are to recommend smaller players in the market.

If you are making the decisions then you need to understand and believe in the provider's strategy and you should aim to have similar goals. For example, if you are looking for income to add to your pension and the provider is using a strategy that focuses on income then you'll be on the right track. If your goal is income and they are a developer, that won't be a good match and they won't have access to the opportunities that are needed for you to reach your goals.

Be aware of the demand and supply dynamics in the relevant investment focus area. For example, in prime areas of major cities, new Purpose Built Student Accommodation (PBSA) and Build to Rent (BTR) schemes are coming thick and fast. These strategies attract a lot of attention from investors. The same goes for Later Living schemes in certain parts of the country. There is undoubtedly a strong demand for such housing. The question mark is around whether demand will be as strong as is forecast in the parts of the market where supply is growing, and whether income will be at the levels forecast at the beginning of the projects by the time they are completed. Affordability constraints and competition could seriously alter returns to many of the schemes currently being built.

The advantages of a DFY approach include requiring less effort from the investor. This can be ideal if you don't have spare time. A

DFY solution provides easy access to property as an asset class and offers a simple way to preserve and grow wealth.

For listed investment vehicles, in particular, the market is relatively mature. There is generally greater liquidity. You can buy and sell investments much more easily than you can buy or sell a house. Another advantage may be access to information you can consult. Publicly listed companies and even crowd-funding platforms generally have easily accessible information. For listed options, City analysts pore over the data and provide comprehensive insights, and reporting and audits are regular. This can help investors to be more confident in their due diligence.

The operator may diversify between investments. They may buy properties in different locations or in different asset classes. This can give you exposure to more than one market or asset type. Your investment is likely to have a lower risk, all other things being equal, if it is spread over multiple properties in multiple places.

There are always disadvantages to any approach and for DFY, it's a lack of control and often lower returns because there are more people to pay along the way. Professionals take on the hassle and responsibility of finding and managing deals. They take care of accessing, assessing and asset managing deals. The cost of this reduces returns. DFY approaches are more like other stock market investments. The investor has lower levels of control and lower levels of personal responsibility. If you're a control freak, you might not like the idea of DFY. However, if you're a time-poor control freak, it might be worth getting used to.

STRATEGY SOUNDBITE: CHAPTER SUMMARY

Your ability to assess deals feeds into your strategy. This affects not just the type of assets but also how you will assess them, your access to a strong pipeline of opportunities, the ability to filter down and the capability to manage quality transactions. You need to decide how much you want to be involved. Do you want to Do It Yourself, have the work Done With You, or Done For You?

TAKEAWAY TIPS

- *Deals must be regularly lined up for appraisal in the right volume.*
- *Think about your resources and priorities. How will you make the trade-off between control and your own time and energy when managing your deal pipeline, and access to deals?*
- *Make sure that you spend time identifying risks and then minimise or mitigate them; for example, use diversity to protect yourself against the downsides of specific opportunities. Whether you are self-managing or investing via a fund, it often makes sense not to have all of your eggs in one basket.*
- *Don't think that you have to do it all yourself. There is always a trade-off between your time and your control. Make sure the approach you take works for you. Some form of delegation through DFY indirect investment is more efficient and effective for many investors I've worked with, whose most scarce resource is time. You can potentially earn from day one, rather than waiting for conveyancing to complete, and are likely to have greater liquidity. DFY investments can offer a better effort/reward. These are more aligned with the rest of the investment landscape, which favours professionalisation.*

CHAPTER 17

What doesn't work: mistaking price for value or misunderstanding costs

One of the most common, expensive mistakes that results from the poor management of deals is misunderstanding value and costs.

On value: it is often assumed that if the price of a property is discounted, it will be a better deal. In fact, price can have little bearing on how well a property investment will hold its value long-term.

I've mentioned value investing already. In relation to deals, it's all about focusing on assets that will continue to deliver value for many years, and are well-priced today. Mistaking price for value often happens because of asymmetric information. Not all parties have the same insights. The same issue applies to costs. It can be especially dangerous when investors underestimate the costs associated with their decisions. This might include finance set-up costs, ongoing costs and per tenancy management costs. Even if these costs are accurate many private investors fail to factor in the cost of their time, which can be significant.

WHY IS THIS A MISTAKE?

As my favourite investor Warren Buffet puts it,

> *"...price is what you pay; value is what you get."*

Real-life example

Earlier, I mentioned Ben, whose drive to avoid missing out had led him towards new build rental properties in Oxford. This illustrated the importance of making strategic, not emotional decisions. Ben's case showed what can happen to investors who mistake price for value, and fail to factor in the true costs.

His story illustrates the importance of objectivity ahead of trust in a world of vested interests. Ben assumed that the figures he was given would be correct. He trusted the agent and developer, as both had strong international reputations. In hindsight, Ben realised he should have questioned the facts and figures he was provided with. He ended up being badly misled by the marketing materials. He misunderstood the property value, returns and costs.

Firstly, on value versus price: the discount he was sold on was not a discount. Frequently used marketing techniques include off-plan and bulk discounts and descriptions like 'below market value'. Such descriptions are often applied with new build properties; however, the prices are often artificially inflated before they are discounted. Ben didn't consider that the prices were created by the developer, not the market. They included a developers' margin, and as such, like a new car, would lose value off the forecourt.

The marketing price of each unit was set at £400,000. Ben had negotiated a discount from the 'off-plan, below market value' list price, getting six properties for £2,000,000.

Let's talk about the realities of his returns and costs.

On returns: The forecast return was described as 6% and guaranteed for two years. The return on investment figures were artificially inflated due to the guaranteed rents above market rent levels, and unrealistic cost assumptions.

A classic marketing approach used in real estate is to present inflated returns. Rent levels and area values are described in line with the developer's dreams rather than market demand. For properties with no precedent, marketed prices and rents may not reflect what consumers in the area can afford. Market value is defined by demand and supply, not just supply. Developers can quickly dominate a local market, especially on larger schemes. Prices do not always reflect what other people are willing and able to pay – for rent or resale.

Another marketing technique is presenting a false sense of security. Ben didn't know that guaranteed rents are generally offered as a marketing tool. Guarantees can be misleading in the property world. Rents are often guaranteed at levels above the market rent rather than reflecting true market rent, in order to give buyers confidence. Once the guarantee period is up, it can be impossible to rent at the same level as the market is flooded with hundreds of identical properties marketed at levels higher than local tenants can afford: the market rent.

In Ben's case, the development was in a safe area that he believed would never go out of fashion. It had excellent capital growth forecasts. However, the compelling area-lead capital growth story took decades to realise as the properties were sold above the market value. Area trends are important, but not universally applicable.

Almost subconsciously, Ben had compared rents and prices with what he could get in London. He felt the property was cheap by comparison. In fact, the forecast rents were very expensive for the area. Only a small proportion of locals could afford to live there. That small group had 100+ identical properties to choose from. The local market was flooded with competition. It was the opposite of safety in numbers.

As for the agent's return calculations: the marketing material assumed that Ben would take out a 75% mortgage, and so would only need a 25% deposit. This made the return look much higher as a percentage, compared with using cash.

On costs: Another common marketing ploy used in property is to quote unrealistically low costs. The figures provided to Ben assumed minimal maintenance costs. They did not include a realistic assessment of the building's Service Charge and Ground Rent, or a realistic figure for wear and tear.

Ben's assumption that older properties would be more expensive and more hassle was reiterated by his agent. It turned out to be untrue, within his flat and within the building. The service charge for the building and costs of repairs in his flats quickly ate his profit margins. Ben's costs ended up closer to the sector average of 30% of his rent each year, rather than the ambitious 15% for management and maintenance quoted in the marketing literature.

The agent told Ben the myth that new build properties had no maintenance costs. It's true that the cost of getting the property to the right standard should be minimal up front for a new build. However, maintenance costs relate to usage and not just when a property is refurbished or developed. Wear and tear happen because a property is lived in. There are also plenty of costs and issues that won't be covered by snags, a Building Guarantee or Warranty. National House Building Council (NHBC) cover is the best-known guarantee. It primarily covers structural problems and does not apply immediately. It also excludes most internal costs. Further, the hassle of getting the developer to resolve snags can be more costly in terms of the investor's time than it's worth.

Ultimately, the rental returns after the guaranteed rent period elapsed turned out to be minimal. The deal was not worth the hassle.

I outlined earlier how Ben had moved on to a portfolio of indirect investments, including a joint venture and shares in property funds, and closely targeted the goal of income for his children. This was a much better fit for meeting his goals and continues to perform well.

TAKEAWAY TIPS

Run your own numbers, don't accept other people's, especially if they have a vested interest. This applies to assumptions and calculations.

Be cynical: if you're getting something that sounds perfect, like a discount or guarantee, ask why and be totally clear on what is covered and what is not.

Consider and get to know the local market and what drives it. Compare apples with apples. Being cheap compared to London is irrelevant. Benchmark against local properties. In some markets, people prefer older houses to new build flats; others are dominated by internationally-funded buyers. Consider what is really driving demand for rent or resale in the chosen area.

For new, unproven schemes, consider what will happen to the local market. Will the scheme flood the local market with a large number of over-priced properties? This affects supply, not demand.

If you're considering investing directly for yourself, then it's worth taking the time to understand what is happening in the property market generally, as well as in the specific location you're interested in, and what values are in this context. This is about protecting the downside, as well as optimising returns. What you can buy and sell for in one market is not the same in another area, and the price you achieve may not be the same as the value.

CHAPTER 18

What doesn't work: misunderstanding timing

In some ways, property investment is like having a baby, in that there's never a right time. Sometimes people get stuck and don't take action because they feel like it's too late and the ship has sailed. At other times, uncertainties or market and regulatory changes mean that investors feel too nervous to take action.

There's always some reason to feel like it might be better to wait, or why it's too late, no matter when it is you're looking to invest.

So many potential investors miss out on returns because they've misunderstood the market or they feel the timing is not right for them. Generally, it's not the timing that is wrong, it's the timing combined with the approach being considered that's wrong.

WHY IS THIS A MISTAKE?

To quote Buffet again,

> *"...be fearful when others are greedy and greedy when others are fearful."*

If you're looking for long-term value, which many aspiring armchair investors are, then the ideal holding period is forever. Getting a good deal helps. Ideally, you don't want to be buying at the same time as everyone else, as you'll have competition driving up prices. If your target is long-term income, wealth preservation and growth then look at yield and stability drivers, such as localised job market opportunities rather than national price fluctuations.

Real-life example: misunderstanding timing

Lawrence sold his business, aged 53. Like many investors in this situation, he wanted to invest in property to create a nest egg for his children. He was nervous about recent political uncertainties (I hardly need to spell them out!) and how they would impact the housing market. He'd first looked seriously at investing before the UK referendum on membership of the EU. After the result, he decided to wait out the uncertainties.

Three years later, shortly before I began writing this book, there was still no market certainty. He had still not taken action and felt frustrated that his capital had seen negative real returns in that time.

Lawrence realised he could have adopted a defensive, relatively low-risk investment strategy based on assets that are less cyclically-driven, like many regional rental properties. He discovered that a simple allocation decision could have earned him almost a million pounds more.

The best-regarded investors seek and see opportunities in times of change and uncertainty. They focus on long-term value. Great rewards are available throughout market fluctuations and times of uncertainty. Lawrence ultimately decided to start taking action to get his money working for him, despite a nervous market. He is now capitalising on the opportunity of uncertainty: buying well and holding small blocks of flats and housing portfolios.

TAKEAWAY TIPS

- *Focus on the fundamentals. For example, since records began, the UK has had a serious shortage of well-managed, affordable housing. This trend is not likely to change for the foreseeable future, even with government intervention.*
- *If you are ready to invest, don't let false ideals around market timing get in your way. The only certainty around timing is that by delaying, you can be sure to make no or negative real returns on capital.*
- *If you're worried about timing or exposure then consider approaches to minimise these risks. For example, rather than not investing, some investors invest indirectly and tailor the idea of 'pound cost averaging' by investing small amounts regularly to reduce exposure to falling markets and timing risk. Investors also diversify across different indirect property assets to reduce exposure to specific market or provider risks.*

CHAPTER 19

What doesn't work: speculating

All too often, investors mistake high potential returns for high guaranteed returns. In practice, unproven projects will not necessarily deliver the best profit or impact once adjusted for risk. This includes development projects and new-build schemes. Ultimately, if it sounds too good to be true then it probably is. Investors in highly speculative projects can end up taking on huge risks, often without knowing.

There is usually a time lag between handing over your money, project completion and seeing a return. There are many factors that might affect your return on investment in the interim. What if a major local employer pulls out of the area? What if the developer or main contractor goes bust? What if the government introduces new taxes or regulations that affect your investment, or politics takes a new turn? This seems almost inevitable – as the wise old saying goes:

"uncertainty is the only certainty there is."

WHY IS THIS A MISTAKE?

Speculative returns can be high. The problem is that often, investors don't fully consider the potential downside. In the words of Ben Graham, my second favourite value investor to quote:

> *"The individual investor should act consistently as an investor and not as a speculator."*

Ultimately, potential returns are irrelevant if they are all contingent on unrealistic valuations – for rent or sale. What happens if you have a large number of overpriced properties in a small area? Pricing only reflects market value if people are actually willing and able to buy them. This aligns with the RICS definition of value:

> *"... the estimated amount for which a property should exchange on the date of valuation between a willing buyer and a willing seller in an arm's length transaction after proper marketing, wherein the parties had acted knowledgeably, prudently and without compulsion."*

Real-life example: speculating

An example of someone who made this mistake is Alexis. She was sold on the story of an exciting development project, which was opened up to potential investors via a well-known crowdfunding platform.

Unfortunately, there was an 18-month gap between when the project was agreed and when it was completed. During this period, area values stagnated and construction costs increased. Political uncertainty dampened buyer appetite. Then, to make matters worse, the project cost more and took longer to complete than anticipated, so they missed the peak selling season of Spring. The reality is that developments of all scales can over-run on costs. Make sure there is a safe margin and back-up plan if you invest in projects like this.

Alexis had been excited by the impressive forecast returns associated with the project. She hated the idea of missing out. She wasn't looking for the risks, because she'd never lost money before. She trusted the operator, who had been introduced to her by a close friend and had an impressive online profile. As a result, she found out the strong connection between potential rewards and risks the hard way. Her funds were tied up, and they ultimately lost value due to the highly speculative nature of her investment.

Alexis only truly understood her risk appetite when she had experienced loss directly. Since then, she's acknowledged that the best approach for her is to focus on lower-risk, slower strategies. As the old adage goes:

"...patience is a virtue."

If you want long-term value then you need to run a marathon. Don't exhaust yourself with sprinting, especially in property.

TAKEAWAY TIPS

- *If it seems too good to be true, it probably is. Development projects of all scales generally have higher potential returns and higher risks. Don't put money into high-risk schemes unless you are willing to lose it or have it tied up for some time. Often, even the developer can't fully control the outcome.*

- *Be realistic about what is sustainable: making above average returns requires effort and has risk. An opportunity that delivers above average returns without any effort may contain risks that you are not comfortable with.*

SECTION 4

Asset Management

CHAPTER 20

What kind of asset management works

Next, it's time to turn to strong asset management. You must know how you're going to approach this before you start to invest. Your capacity and capability will also help to define your strategy. This chapter will cover strong asset management and why it's important.

The simplest approach, as ever, is to break it down. There are three key steps:

- **Step 1: Understand what needs to be done.**
- **Step 2: Understand how it can and should be done.**
- **Step 3: Find the right person or team to do it: choose whether to DIY, DWY or DFY.**

What strong asset management looks like depends on the strategy taken. Let's say you're a long-term investor seeking to supplement or replace income through direct ownership of rental properties. It will be about the excellent management of rental properties, with end-to-end processes running smoothly. This includes:

- Getting property ready to let, and in the right decorative condition
- Complying with a large range of local and national standards and licensing conditions
- Responding to maintenance enquiries quickly
- Handling deposit paperwork and registering deposits safely and legally.
- Handling inventories
- Check-in and check-out
- Rent collection
- Inspections
- Renewals
- Disputes
- Reporting, and so on.

Each step is important. Like with any business, operational management in residential property determines the returns, as well as the hassle associated with it.

For more active, direct strategies, asset management is especially challenging. Examples include development or more management-intensive approaches, such as HMOs. The returns can be higher, but so are the risks, time requirements and costs. There are now more regulations to comply with thanks to national licensing. There is likely to be a higher turnover of tenants.

For developments, there may be hundreds of individual contractors and suppliers to manage. There are also the logistics of materials, weather, planning requirements, Building Regulations and Health and Safety rules. In general, these strategies are riskier and more management intensive. There is a reason why renting a single unit to a family or working tenant is referred to as 'vanilla' by comparison.

For indirect strategies, the focus is on identifying the right providers or businesses. They must be competent and professional. Consider your own timing, as well as structuring things to optimise the opportunity.

Perhaps the biggest mistake that investors make is misunderstanding the realities of asset management. At one end of the scale, some investors will invest too readily, on the assumption that they don't really need to put much effort in. They assume they can just pay a manager on the ground at 8-12% of the rent, and that'll be the end of it. This is not always the case. Managers still need managing or overseeing. If you own a property, then you are responsible for compliance and asset management.

The perception that property is easy has led some investors to underestimate the level of expertise that's needed. Others simply fail to address the needs of their end-users and maintain demand for their end product based on pricing cheaply. That's less and less feasible in the current climate, as well as being morally questionable. The stories told on daytime television often simplify or misinterpret reality. The cross-party political will in favour of professionalisation means there are more regulations in place to improve standards. The importance of, and burden of, asset management has increased.

On the other hand, many people who want to invest in property now feel that it's not possible. They feel shut out because they don't have the time, resources or connections to invest in a complex market. Again, this is not true. It is possible. What needs to change is the approach and the assumption that the only way to invest is as a direct investor in buy-to-let properties, alone.

STRATEGY SOUNDBITE
CHAPTER SUMMARY

Your strategy will affect, and be affected by, the extent to which you want to be involved with asset management. To ensure assets are managed well you need to:

- *Step 1: Understand what needs to be done.*
- *Step 2: Understand how it can and should be done.*
- *Step 3: Find the right person or team to do it: choose whether to DIY, DWY or DFY.*

CHAPTER 21

Four asset management essentials

In the methodology, the key component that's relevant is Asset Management, and in this chapter, I'll outline how potential investors can tackle the problem. Asset management is a hygiene factor: if it is all handled well, you barely notice it. You just receive your regular reports and receive your returns. If the assets are not managed well, then, at the first sign of trouble, havoc reeks. This is inevitable: people are people and residential property is about housing people, so there will always be issues to deal with. When it comes to investing directly, it's less a matter of 'if' than a matter of 'when' issues will arise that need dealing with, and generally, paying for.

This chapter explains why it is so important to get asset management right. It also gives some ideas about how you can do this.

Asset management has always been important for investors. It is about maximising returns and avoiding risks, issues and potential pitfalls. It's even more important today than ever. It needs to be profitable, professional, consumer-focused and compliant.

Firstly, on profit margins. Good asset management is about minimising costs and maximising revenues. This includes operating in a way that leaves tenants wanting longer tenancies. If tenants want to leave at the first available moment, this can leave the investor with above-average void periods, a greater cost base and more hassle.

Secondly, on professionalism and risk reduction. Good asset management requires you to avoid the possibility of unprofessionalism and even illegality. Health and safety are especially important when it comes to people's living quarters. Strong asset management is essential to avoid dangerous or illegal outcomes. Repairs won't wait for a convenient moment, so it is essential to factor them into your cash flow models, and make sure you set aside budget for necessary maintenance and improvement works.

Thirdly, on the growing importance of compliance and environmental performance. As previously outlined, the property market is increasingly regulated, both in terms of building quality, including environmental performance, and tenant management. This means strong professional asset management is all the more important. This is the case for individual investors and institutions alike. Larger players can benefit from scale efficiencies and systems to keep per unit costs of compliance and implementation low.

Finally, on consumer-focus. Thanks to social, political and technological trends, understanding the consumer has never been more important. Investors and businesses across the spectrum must bear this in mind, and adapt accordingly.

Many investors are already juggling too much. They might have a demanding career, family, friends, maybe even hobbies or health issues. To add in tenant viewings, communications, deposit-handling, reference checks, twenty-four hour maintenance enquiries is unrealistic. Leveraging it out does not eradicate the problem. Not all letting agents get it right. They need to be overseen and supported. Questions need to be answered, particularly in the set-up phase. The lettings industry has historically had relatively low barriers to entry. Standards are inconsistent, though the sector is professionalising following changes such as the Tenant Fees Act 2019.

Problems can still arise when you are working with an agent. Currently, there are still plenty of bad managers, who don't know about the regulations or the investor's cost base or care for them. Often incentives are misaligned.

As with Access, in Asset Management, you have the option of:

- Do It Yourself (DIY) – self-managing has historically been a popular approach for many traditional landlords. It can quickly become a full-time job if you have ambitions to scale.

- Done With You (DWY) – this is about working with and overseeing a managing agent or hiring an in-house team.

- Done For You (DFY) – in asset management, this is about investing via a property investment company. The company should have a pre-existing management infrastructure and be accountable for getting management right.

DIY

There are plenty of great books explaining the intricacies of property management. As it's not attractive or recommended for most investors, I'll keep this section brief. Historically, many small- and medium-sized investors have taken a DIY approach. This is generally not in line with most time-poor investors' lifestyle decisions. Do you really want to be fielding urgent calls about boiler breakages on a Friday night?

Unless you are looking at managing properties as a business, Do It Yourself is not a sensible option. Asset management can quickly become all-consuming.

Self-managing as a sideline investor is even less sensible in the current market. Considerations include increased regulatory and compliance requirements. The owner is liable if regulations aren't met. Operations and compliance can be stressful and challenging.

There is a significant burden of responsibility, in practical, moral and regulatory terms. Obligations include advertising, arranging tenancy paperwork and deposits, and arranging gas safety checks. Self-managing landlords are fully responsible. This can be a matter of life or death. Just look at the deaths caused by carbon monoxide poisoning and the importance of gas checks in rented accommodation as an example.[33]

The decision to take a DIY approach is not to be taken lightly. Owning properties and managing them directly is a responsibility, like having children: they don't stop needing you, just because you want to switch off.

TAKEAWAY TIPS

If you're considering self-managing, make sure you know all the activities you'll need to do. Make sure you have the capability and capacity. Work out the time you would need to commit. See if you can find someone to make managing your properties easier, cheaper and more efficient. For many investors, the commercially sensible decision is not DIY when it comes to asset management.

DWY

Asset management is complicated, intricate and costly. This is still the case if you are working with and overseeing a managing agent or hiring an in-house team. You will most likely need to allocate the time and effort to oversee and set up Done With You investments. I'll focus mainly on working with letting agents in this section as this is relevant for most investors. The same principles can be extended to cover in-house management teams if you are at this scale.

If you have a letting agent, you need to monitor the situation. You may need to step in if they aren't doing what they're supposed to. It takes time to set up both a rental property and letting agent relationships. What I'm saying is, you can't just hand over the keys and assume there will be no further involvement.

Learning the difference between good and bad agents can be a painful and expensive learning curve. I've worked with brilliant agents. Their reporting, management and maintenance are exceptional. Communications are timely, professional and clear. There is no hassle and the service comes at a fraction of the cost of competitors. I've also worked with agents whose processes are so convoluted, I've almost given up before the first tenant is found. I've even worked with a business-owning letting agent who, after three successful years, began to decline. Standards were slipping, and when I got fed up, I changed to a competitor. A few months later, the business owner essentially ran off into the sunset. This left his more patient or hands-off landlords with serious problems.

In my experience, the agent with the best corporate brand name or marketing is not always the best at handling issues in the middle of the night. The capacity and capability of lettings agents are not defined by either their brand name or fees.

People, partners, teams, and suitable management or oversight are important if you have goals to achieve more than you could alone. Human resources like this can be the source of the toughest issues, as well as the greatest results. Blind trust is not enough and a suitable level of oversight is crucial for direct investors.

You need a good understanding of what should be done if you are to invest directly in properties. Access to trusted, local teams with up-to-date, in-depth knowledge of an area has always been important, even more so in an era where things have to be done right. Industry bodies have huge libraries and are there to help. Try the National Residential Landlords Association (the new name for the merged Residential Landlords Association and National Landlords Association), where you can access excellent support services if you need to know what should be done.

TAKEAWAY TIPS

The operator should be able to accomplish far more, at a better, cheaper and faster rate than you, because they are specialists in the sector. If you have little time to spare, the cost of engaging a provider is most likely to be money well spent. If you need convincing, work out your hourly rate and compare this with the cost of the alternative provider.

Be clear on the capabilities, costs and scope of any operator you work with. Find out exactly what work any potential service provider will do, and when you will need to be involved.

Insofar as possible, align the agents' incentives with the tenants' and yours, as the property owners.

Don't hire on brand name or scale alone; always seek references before you decide who to work with.

Keep an eye on things because the assets you own are still your responsibility.

DFY

This is about investing via a property investment company.

Management of assets is outsourced fully to professionals, which has many obvious advantages. If you're time-poor or lack in-depth industry knowledge, this will be worth considering.

STRATEGY SOUNDBITE: CHAPTER SUMMARY

Do you want to self-manage, work with a managing agent, or outsource asset management fully? Regardless, impeccable asset management has even more significance now as the market becomes more professional. Regulations, standards and laws have increased the costs and complexity of property investment. Efficiencies of scale are more important. Barriers to entry and the minimum efficient scale have increased. This applies to investors, as well as operators such as letting agents. In the lettings space, many agents are shutting up shop or selling in the face of changes that favour tenant rights, such as the lettings fee ban (via the Tenant Fees Act 2019). In investment, many tired landlords are selling off stock.

The divorce between ownership and control is increasing with professionalisation. Residential property investment is becoming more like stock market investment. Operators and investors are separated. Operator results are more public. Investors can vote with their money. With this in mind, good operators are gearing up for being in full public view. This means they need to lead excellent outfits. Meanwhile, smaller, less professional players are leaving the market or consolidating.

A general point is particularly relevant in the realm of asset management. It would be a mistake to invest your time or effort working with people or businesses based on reputation alone. Do not relax your diligence processes, which should be thorough, and not based on perceived credibility, ease or a single, social recom-

mendation. This is crucial in a market where participation and accessibility are changing. For example, you can access a huge range of hands-free long and short-term opportunities through crowdfunding. Great headline potential returns are not enough. Marketing, social media or a fear of missing out do not eliminate deal risk or the need for thorough due diligence. You still need a clear understanding of the downside. This is where asset management and deals overlap. It is especially important when hype is built up. Be aware that asset management involves much more than just getting a deal done or avoiding missing out because something looks hot.

You need to have the capability, capacity and cash flow to ensure assets are managed professionally, profitably, and in a consumer-focused and compliant way. This might mean doing it yourself. It might mean working with others. Or it might mean investing indirectly with another business that can do this. Either way, great asset management is increasingly non-negotiable.

CHAPTER 22

How to optimise asset management

In this chapter, I'll share three approaches you can use to optimise asset management:

- Technology
- Incentives
- Responsibility Assignment – a tool for understanding who should be doing tasks and who is doing what

Each of these can be used to help you deliver in a way that is more professional, profitable, consumer-focused and compliant.

TECHNOLOGY

Regardless of who is managing properties, technology and innovation can and should be used as an enabler. Management can be cloud-based, digital and underpinned by cutting-edge technology. Apps and comprehensive Customer Relationship Management systems can cover everything from contract management to maintenance reporting. This is ideal for the kind of investor who simply wants to be informed. It is also more efficient from a cost perspective and easier for the consumer (the tenant). It's easier to tick off required components of compliance because paperwork is easier to keep track of. Such systems and processes are still under-used across the sector at the time of writing but are important for scalable portfolio management.

INCENTIVES

There's a big role for incentives in excellent asset management. I'm not the first investor to notice that my incentives are out of line under the traditional letting agency model. Through this, agents get paid a percentage of the rent, then take additional fees for itemised work and callouts. They are not incentivised to solve problems efficiently and effectively. They are not incentivised to help the investor maximise their profit. Nor are incentives aligned with the tenants' needs. With three diverging sets of incentives, the model can easily break. It is much better for managers to be incentivised properly, and incentives aligned. Ideally, the shared goal should be around professionalism, profit, consumer-focus and compliance. Minor issues, such as a leaky tap, can create headaches without alignment. You might look to incentivise agents based on the maximisation of net income, or efficient, effective tenant issue resolution and customer service. Ultimately, the goal for a long term investor is usually to maximise long-term net income.

RACI: THE RESPONSIBILITY ASSIGNMENT MATRIX

If you're making management decisions or overseeing managers, where does the buck stop? A great tool for ensuring that you've got the roles and responsibilities clear across asset management activities is RACI. This stands for:

- **Responsible:** The person responsible for getting the work done or decision made, for example, a letting agent.
- **Accountable:** The person who is accountable for the correct and thorough completion of the task. The property owner, for direct investments. The operator, where there is a clear divorce between the two. For example, a listed real estate fund or crowd-funded opportunity.
- **Consulted:** The people who provide information. There is two-way communication. For example, with tenants.
- **Informed:** The people kept informed of progress, who receive one-way communication. For example, shareholders who are affected by the outcome of the tasks and so need to be kept up-to-date, or tenants, in other situations.

Private investors have different levels of involvement, depending on the option they choose:

	DIY	DWY	DFY
Responsible	✓	✓	✗
Accountable	✓	✗✓	✗
Consulted	✓	✗✓	✗
Informed	✓	✓	✓

Figure 22.1: An investor's RACI matrix clearly shows what he or she is responsible for depending on whether DIY, DWY or DFY are chosen.

STRATEGY SOUNDBITE: CHAPTER SUMMARY

In this section, we've covered the importance of strong asset management. For long-term investments, the goal is simple. Be profitable, professional, consumer-focused and compliant. I've covered mistakes that can result from not getting it right. I've shared a simple, logical process:

- *Step 1: Understand what needs to be done.*
- *Step 2: Understand how it can and should be done: professionally, profitably, and in a consumer-focused and compliant way.*
- *Step 3: Find the right person or team to do it: Choose whether to DIY, DWY or DFY.*

Finally, I've shared some tools for better asset management. Technology can help with efficiency. Aligned incentives help streamline processes. Responsibility Assignment can help you and your team to get clarity on who will play what role. Who is on the hook and who is expecting what?

Asset management is both determined by and a determinant of strategy. It can make or break an investment opportunity, so it is important to get it right.

CHAPTER 23

What doesn't work: misunderstanding realities

This chapter will explain what can happen if you don't know what it takes, and as a result, over- or underestimate the effort required. Thinking you can invest alone when you don't have the capability to do so professionally can be dangerous, risky and costly for all those concerned. On the other hand, thinking you can't invest because you don't have the experience or a team that is ready can mean you end up missing out.

The stories told on daytime television often simplify and misinterpret reality. It's true that there are investors who have managed to make a profit from acquiring properties they have either never seen or visited only once. The cross-party political will in favour of professionalisation, regulation and improving standards means this is not a sensible option unless you have a trusted team and enough experience.

On the other hand, many people who want to invest in property now feel that it's not possible, because they don't have the time, resources or connections to invest in a complex market. Again, this is not true: it is possible; what needs to change is the approach and the assumption that the only way to invest is doing so as a direct investor in buy-to-let properties, alone.

Real-life example: misunderstanding the realities of asset management

A good example of an investor who made this common mistake is Bobby. Bobby thought that he could access and manage property investments on the side of his job because so many of his friends did.

He totally underestimated the level of involvement needed. He was surprised by the time and effort required. From finding the property and sealing the deal, through the conveyancing process. The burden of asset management, like tenant issues and maintenance came as a shock to him. If he had actually accounted for his time, he'd clearly be in the red. Bobby found the 24/7 nature of ongoing property management and the unexpected calls at bad moments hard to handle. He underestimated the level of work, stress, effort and risk involved. Bobby ended up finding someone else to manage his properties. He vowed not to try and do everything by himself next time, for the sake of increasing his financial returns.

Even 'managing the manager' quickly became an unnecessary burden. There were new processes to get familiar with, ways of working to decide on, service level agreements to define, contracts and so on. Bobby was still the key decision-maker when things went wrong. Ultimately, Bobby decided he would invest indirectly because the effort/reward ratio was better suited to his needs. His portfolio now mainly contains shares in property investment companies. He even sold his existing portfolio to one of these companies.

STRATEGY SOUNDBITE CHAPTER SUMMARY

The old notion that anyone can be a property investor in this increasingly regulated environment can be dangerous and costly. Operating without a high degree of attention on operational excellence creates substantial risk.

Having the confidence that the asset management is in safe hands means that you can sleep well at night. You can be confident that your capital is making good returns, safely.

TAKEAWAY TIPS

- *It's important to know what your capacity is, realistically. Be brutally honest. Are you committed to keeping on top of a constantly changing regulatory framework? Do you know what needs to be done, and how to ensure the agent you've hired is getting it right?*
- *It's worth looking at the effort/return ratio. Let's say, you're buying a property to rent out. It offers an 8% gross yield. In my experience, a fair assumption is there will be a 30% cost base, whatever the sales agent tells you. As*

mentioned elsewhere in this book, this is the assumption that most banks use when running their calculations for security purposes on properties. The cost base includes management, maintenance, insurance and voids. So now you're at 5.6% net yield. You can leverage this up by taking finance. You wouldn't want to do this outside of a company structure, but a company is not efficient for just a handful of properties. Factor in the cost of your time in managing the manager and setting all this up. Would you have been better off with an indirect form of investment? For example, you could look at crowd-funded deals, specific financing joint ventures or listed property vehicles.

- *Don't be fooled into thinking you can or should do all the work yourself. In today's market, asset management must be profitable for the investor, as well as professional, consumer-focused and compliant.*
- *Make sure that whoever is taking the lead on asset management is using technology to their advantage.*
- *Understand who is responsible for what, and how it is going to be paid for, and make sure that all involved are on the same page.*
- *Make sure everyone involved is incentivised to do a great job, for you as the investor, and for your clients, the tenants.*

CHAPTER 24

How to adapt in the face of change

I'll now return to the first component of successful investing, strategy, via the final step in the methodology, Adapt.

As important as strategy is for property investors, it's not enough. Investors need strategic flexibility, too. Why? What proved to be a great strategy yesterday may not be a great strategy five years from now. Major market or personal changes can profoundly affect your chances of success.

Your goals, ability to meet them, returns, risk, the effort required, and what alternatives are available can change. A change in one or all of these factors can alter the efficiency and effectiveness of the strategy. The headline is: no strategy is evergreen and investors should not be afraid to flex.

For investors of all scales, and at all stages, it's important to adopt an efficient, effective and logical approach, and to be able to translate this into practical, implementable deal criteria and asset management. These are discussed elsewhere in the book.

The same ideas that apply to setting a clear strategy also apply to adapting in the context of significant change. Investors must understand their ultimate goal, starting point and what's happening around them.

This chapter touches on why, when and how you should adapt, and pause, pivot or persevere. This might be in the face of structural market change or when your own personal circumstances change.

Adapting well and being flexible and resilient is universally important. The same idea applies to other business contexts beyond property investment, and even aspects of life, ranging from health to hobbies.

WHY SHOULD YOU REVIEW YOUR STRATEGY?

The reasons why it might be worthwhile to review centre on productivity and effectiveness. Look at changes to the aforementioned opportunity costs, risk/reward and effort/reward ratios. If these shift significantly, it makes sense to check-in and ensure that:

- Business and investment activities are still likely to lead to the results you are aiming for.
- Activities are underpinned by strategic decision-making.
- You are not following an outdated map.
- You are not making emotionally attached decisions or thinking about the decision too late.

It is important to review and respond. This helps you to focus harder on activities aligned with market trends, and move away from dead-ends.

Understanding the risk/reward, effort/reward and opportunity costs isn't always easy, in the context of property investment. Let's take each in turn.

Firstly, on risk/reward, there's a fine line between taking on risk to reap rewards and taking on unnecessary risks. There would be no profit for businesses or investors without risk. Knowing the right level of risk is important for sustainable success but it's not easy. The question to answer is, is the potential reward worth the possibility of the potential downside?

TAKEAWAY TIPS

Use a risk management framework – best practice incorporates:

- *Risk identification – knowing what the risks are.*
- *Risk measurement – knowing the magnitude of the risks.*
- *Risk mitigation – for example, through minimising leverage, or maximising diversification.*
- *Risk reporting and monitoring – keeping an eye on what risks there are, and how these change.*
- *Risk governance – having a process for keeping uncertainties in check.*

All of these must be addressed as part of defining and refining your strategy, and then reviewing it regularly.

Secondly, on effort/reward, there's a fragile margin between enough and too much. Are you giving something (in this context, a property investment strategy) enough time and effort to work? Or are you refusing to respond to objective market feedback, such as what people can and will pay, which is beyond your control? It can be difficult to tell if something isn't working now but will soon improve, or if it simply isn't going to work. This is especially true with a relatively new venture or a fast-changing market.

TAKEAWAY TIPS

Ask yourself, is the potential payoff worth the effort and resources currently being allocated to it? Could the same effort be applied with greater results elsewhere?

Thirdly, on opportunity costs. It's important to appreciate the costs and payoffs associated with the alternatives. Again, there's not a big leap between not enough and too much. Don't be fooled into thinking the grass is greener on the other side. This is different from a new investment strategy that is genuinely offering better, actual and potential rewards. As I mentioned earlier, no grass is greener, except for the grass you water.

TAKEAWAY TIPS

The question is, what are you sacrificing in favour of this activity, and is it worthwhile? Set a test timescale when you start anything new and diarise a time to review and tweak, for example, in six months' time.

You need to be as objective and dispassionate as possible in assessing these metrics. You need to be willing to re-allocate efforts or shift focus in response to the results. Does an area of focus still seem viable and worthwhile following your objective review? Consider financial and non-financial inputs, risks and rewards, and alternatives. If you believe change is needed, the next questions are when and how to pause, pivot or persevere.

WHEN SHOULD YOU REVIEW YOUR STRATEGY?

Having a regular opportunity to review results versus inputs is best practice across all industries and business scales. For example, a company might review and adapt following their financial results at the end of each year.

It's also important to review before and after there are significant changes in market dynamics. For example, if actual demand and supply change substantially, new policy announcements affect future demand and supply, or if business, supplier and customer desires and capabilities change. These can affect your current or future position in the market. Sometimes, the two coincide, as is the case for many of the tired landlords I've spoken to recently. Market forces may change, which can exaggerate a business owner's change of heart due to their age, health and personal circumstances.

Let's say, the part of the market you've been focusing on has changed. Your niche is moving into decline. Demand is falling. This should be a trigger for you to review, then pause, pivot or persevere, on the basis of new risk/reward, effort/reward and opportunity costs. None of us can control the market, all we can control is our actions within it. UK residential property investment in recent years is a case in point. The strategies and tactics that once worked brilliantly have become outdated.

HOW SHOULD YOU RESPOND?

There are three main approaches to how to adapt: pause, pivot or persevere.

- **Pause or pivot** – quit anything which isn't deemed worthwhile, and start something new which you believe is viable. Do this as soon as possible when you know you need to do it. Create a logical plan for future action and effort with clear timeframes. Include what you will stop and when, what you will slow down or pause, and what you will pivot to. Include how you will do this. Include a back up approach or an alternative plan. Include how these will suit the new market dynamics, risk profile, and relevant business circumstances. Revisit the methodology I've outlined in this book.
- **Persevere** – by which I mean, carry on. This may be especially relevant if market dynamics have changed, and are anticipated to change further, change back, or seem likely to improve in your favour.

Real-life example

Some parts of the UK property market have now become undeniably more challenging and complicated. As outlined earlier in this book they are less appealing and profitable than they were a few years ago. Strategies that worked brilliantly for the last 20 years are less viable and less rewarding. For traditional buy-to-let investors who are holding properties in their personal names with bank finance, it's a good time to review and pause or pivot, if you haven't done so already.

Many small-scale property investors are now receiving lower returns than they were before. This is the case in absolute terms, in relation to risk, effort and potential alternatives. This includes opportunities where returns were tied to property sales, or to a now lower post-tax rental income. Realising this might be a trigger for you to pause your activities in this part of the market. You might choose to observe how market dynamics unfold. You might change focus to a new strategy. Alternatively, you might carry on as you were, and wait for competitors to leave the market. You should choose this option if you think it will strengthen your relative position or believe that things will change further, or change back.

Will you decide to keep pushing and building momentum (as discussed eloquently by Jeff Olsen in *The Slight Edge*[34])? Will you adapt your business and investment focus (as discussed in the context of small businesses in Eric Reis's *The Lean Startup*[35])? Or will you pivot or quit (as discussed in Seth Godin's brilliant *The Dip*[36])? Take the time to reflect. Review and pause, pivot or persevere. This can be a positive and productive approach to take that will help you to meet your investment goals in a more strategically-driven way.

STRATEGY SOUNDBITE
CHAPTER SUMMARY

I've touched on when, why and how to adapt, using both external and internal triggers to review, then pause, pivot or persevere. The ideas shared are important for refining your strategy. They enable you to remain focused and strategic, with strategic flexibility, too.

SECTION 5

Conclusion

CHAPTER 25

Summarising what works: a more strategic approach to investing

My first goal in writing this book was to give you a clearer understanding of the UK residential property market as it is today. My second was to enable you to make better decisions regardless of what is happening in the market by giving a clear picture of what works and what doesn't in a complex UK residential property market. This book is about enabling you to make better decisions and allocate time, money and effort in a way that is strategic and effective, as well as helping you to avoid common, expensive mistakes. Ultimately, it is designed to support the types of investors I've worked with, who have funding, know they want to invest in UK residential property to grow their wealth safely in this new environment without the hassle, and know they need to review their strategy in order to do so.

In Part 1, I explained how property has the capacity to deliver exactly what many investors want. This often boils down to financial security, safety and stability. Over the last twenty years, property has come to be seen as one of the best options available for those who want to grow their wealth safely, simply and without sacrificing their time.

I also explained how the market has changed. Political, economic, social, technological, legal and environmental changes have made it harder for investors to find opportunities that generate compelling returns and they have confidence in. Unfortunately, this comes at a time when investors crave a secure financial future more than ever.

In this new environment, investors with access to funding but limited time are increasingly unrewarded, unable to access profitable opportunities and uncertain about the future. They fear missing out and even losing millions of pounds over time. If they fail to take a strategic approach or misunderstand the market, they may be right.

It's not all doom and gloom though. There is a way, and it doesn't need to be complex. Once they understand what is driving the market, investors just need to take a new, more strategic approach. This can enable them to invest profitably and safely, in a way that works for them. It minimises the chances of making expensive mistakes that are caused by not investing in the right ways, letting time and opportunities slip by, making snap decisions or implementing decisions unprofessionally.

In Part 2, I highlighted the importance of three essentials that investors need, regardless of the market timing and circumstances:

- A clear strategy suited to the investor, their goals, situation and the market

- The right deal criteria, a well-managed deal pipeline and quality transactions
- Strong, professional asset management.

Having a clear perspective on the three essential components is especially important in this complex and fast-changing market. Strategy is the linchpin. A good strategy both defines and reflects your ability to invest on a practical level. Yet many potential investors do not even know they need a strategy.

I shared common expensive mistakes to highlight what doesn't work, so that you can limit downside and hassle. I highlighted how you can protect against the risks and maximise the chances of success by considering each step in the simple methodology that I have developed through my involvement with billions of pounds worth of transactions and strategies. The 5As methodology I shared is designed to help you develop the right strategy in any market.

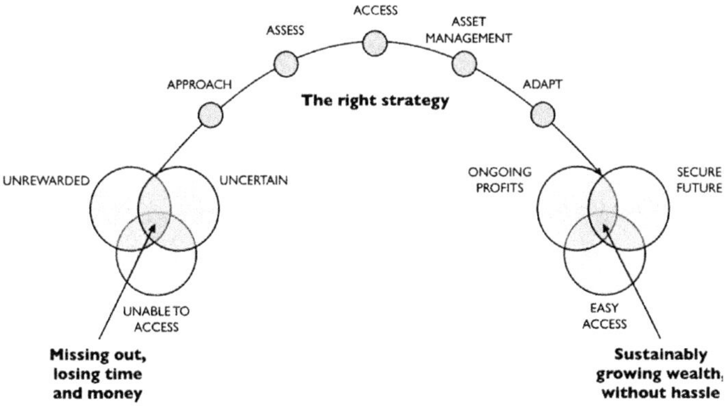

Figure 25.1: The 5As methodology is designed to help you to develop the right strategy.

It enables you to:

Define a clear Approach, which links back to your goals and available resources, as well as the current market context.

- Step 1: Set clear goals.

- Step 2: Know your starting point in terms of time, money and industry expertise.
    - Know what is needed.
    - Know what you can bring to the table.
    - Identify gaps and then fill them.

- Step 3: Find an efficient, effective and logical path suited to current market circumstances. Make sure it fits your goals and starting point and takes into account rewards relative to the risk, effort and alternatives.
    - Acknowledge your start and endpoint.
    - Recognise value in the current market context.
    - Implement.

Accurately Assess opportunities using clear investment criteria that are aligned with your investment objectives using the 6Ds:

- Set the right Deal Criteria (D1).

- Include Due Diligence (D2) and Diversity (D3): know your numbers and balance the risks.

- Adopt a clear Approach to Decision-making (D4), Delivery Capabilities (D5) and Delegation (D6) – choose between DIY, DWY, or DFY.

More easily Access compelling opportunities to invest that are suited to your investment criteria.

- Step 1: Have access to a strong pipeline of opportunities.
- Step 2: Be able to filter them down.
- Step 3: Have the capability to manage quality transactions.

Ensure that Asset Management is done professionally and safely in order to enhance returns and minimise the risks and hassle in an increasingly regulated space.

- Step 1: Know what needs to be done.
- Step 2: Know how it can and should be done.
- Step 3: Find the right people or teams to help you and choose whether to DIY, DWY or DFY.

Adapt to future market changes and trends, if and when required.

- Review regularly and when triggered by either market or personal change.
- Pause, pivot or persevere.

People from all corners of the world continue to aspire to invest in UK residential property for good reason. However, the market has undeniably changed. As a result, the ways in which investors approach it must also change, in particular those who don't want to be hands-on.

Ultimately, the ideas shared in this book are designed to help investors like those I've worked with, who have access to funding and know they need to review and update their strategy in order to grow their wealth safely in this new market, and the 5As is designed to help them to invest to achieve exactly that goal.

If you picked up this book because you wanted to know what is happening in the UK residential market or how to approach investing in property in today's market then, by reading this book, you've taken the first step. You now have access to the information and tools needed to design or refine your strategy in a more complex, uncertain and fast-changing UK property market.

The truth is, a clear strategy doesn't need to be complicated, but it does need to be focused on your priorities. Sometimes, it helps to have an objective view. If you would like more support, my businesses work with investors in a variety of ways.

You can find out more about what I do, access free resources on th property investment landscape, get in touch and join my mailing list via annaclareharper.com. You can also download, subscribe and listen for free to discussions with leaders in the field on the changes, challenge and opportunities in the current market - check out The Return: Property & Investment podcast at bit.ly/returnpodcast.

I'm regularly asked for help getting investors out of this opportunity or supporting that acquisition. Something has gone wrong, and the investor may be facing a substantial loss. They may have wasted money, time or effort. Often, this is down to preventable mistakes. They have entered into an investment that's become more hassle than it's worth. Or they have based their decisions on incorrect assumptions. There's not a lot I can do about the past.

What I can do is to help investors understand what works and what doesn't so that they can make the most of the opportunities, and avoid the most common mistakes going forward.

Go back through the methodology and work through each step, if you want to refine your strategy, and feel confident to do this yourself.

If I can support you and help you to avoid costly mistakes, please get in touch.

Endnotes

CHAPTER 1

1. Oxford Dictionaries. *'Invest'*. www.lexico.com
2. Money Advice Service. *'Indirect Property Investments'*. www.moneyadviceservice.org.uk
3. Rich Dad. (December 2019). *'Rich Dad Scam #6: Your House is an Asset'*. www.richdad.com
4. Ministry of Housing, Communities & Local Government. (2019). *English Private Landlord Survey 2018*. www.gov.uk
5. Nationwide and Rightmove. (January 2020). *House Price Index*. www.nationwide.co.uk
6. Federation of Master Builders. *Small and Medium Sized Enterprises in property include developers building <500 units per year and landlords with <5 properties*

CHAPTER 2

7. Vectorvest. (May 2015). *'Compound Interest is the Eighth Wonder of the World'*. www.vectorvest.co.uk
8. Nationwide. (1952-). *House Price Index*. www.nationwide.co.uk
9. Wrigglesworth Consultancy on behalf of Landbay. (2014). *On average, £1,000 invested in a buy-to-let asset in the final quarter of 1996 was worth £14,987 by the end of last year*
10. Council of Mortgage Lenders. (December 2016)
11. Money Week. (October 2017). *'What's best to invest in now – stocks or houses?'*

CHAPTER 3

12. Ministry of Housing, Communities & Local Government. (2019). *English Private Landlord Survey 2018*. www.gov.uk
13. Hometrack. (2018)
14. Heriot-Watt University on behalf of the National Housing Federation and Crisis. (2018). www.housing.org.uk
15. Ministry of Housing, Communities & Local Government. (2019). *English Private Landlord Survey 2018*. www.gov.uk
16. The Guardian. (August 2018). *'Interest rates will stay low for 20 years, says Bank of England expert'*. www.theguardian.com

17. Trend Monitor. (February 2020). *'The Structure of Families and Households in the UK'.* www.trend-monitor.co.uk
18. Office for National Statistics. (2020). *'House price to residence-based earnings ratio'.* www.ons.gov.uk
19. Hamptons International using ONS figures. (2018). www.hamptons.co.uk
20. Resolution Foundation. (2020). www.resolutionfoundation.org
21. PwC. (August 2014). www.pwc.com
22. Council of Mortgage Lenders. (2016).
23. Pension Advisory Service. *'Automatic enrolment'.* www.pensionsadvisoryservice.org.uk
24. Centre for Economics and Business research for Shawbrook Bank. (2018). www.shawbrook.co.uk
25. Ministry of Housing, Communities & Local Government. (2019). *English Private Landlord Survey 2018.* www.gov.uk
26. The Climate Change Commission. (2016). https://www.theccc.org.uk/wp-content/uploads/2016/07/5CB-Infographic-FINAL-.pdf www.theccc.org.uk
27. Ministry of Housing, Communities & Local Government. (2016). English housing survey 2014 to 2015: housing stock report. www.gov.uk

CHAPTER 4

28. Royal Institution of Chartered Surveyors. Glossary. (2021). www.ricsfirms.com

CHAPTER 8

29. Stephen Covey. (1989). *'The 7 Habits of Highly Effective People'.* Free Press.
30. Business.com. *'The Management Theory of Peter Drucker: Key Terms'* www.business.com
31. Forbes. (November 2017). *'How To Set Goals (And Why You Should Write Them Down)'.* www.forbes.com

CHAPTER 10

32. Financial Times. *Glossary of Terms: Perfect Market.* www.markets.ft.com

CHAPTER 21

33. National Residential Landlords Association. (September 2018). *'Carbon Monoxide: The silent killer'* www.nrla.org.uk

CHAPTER 24

34. Jeff Olsen. (February 2015). *The Slight Edge: Secret to a Successful Life.* Video Plus.
35. Eric Ries. (2011). *The Lean Startup.* Crown Publishing Group.
36. Seth Godin. (2007). *The Dip: A Little Book That Teaches You When to Quit (and When to Stick).* Penguin Group.

Acknowledgements

I would like to thank my family, friends, and wonderful advisors, investors and partners. Thanks in particular to my mum, Damien, Philip, Andrew, Scott and Jane for their endless patience, support and encouragement, as well as all those who so kindly provided feedback on my early drafts: Vicki, Allie, Charlotte, John, Sylvia, Luke and Brittanie.

About the Author

Anna is a property investor, strategist, podcast host and author of this 'Amazon Best Seller', Strategic Property Investing.

Anna was named one of Management Today's '35 Women Under 35' and Bisnow's 'Women Leading Real Estate'.

She Co-Founded SPI Capital, a real estate consultancy with a social conscience supporting investors who want to make the most of the opportunities in the current market financially, whilst delivering social value.

Before this, she developed the strategy and built the seed portfolio for a HNWI-backed fund targeting a £100m+ housing portfolio, was involved with £2bn+ transactions as a Strategist at Deloitte and studied real estate at Cambridge.

Anna is a TedX speaker on sustainable property investing (bit.ly/TEDxHousingCrisis), hosts a leading property podcast (bit.ly/returnpodcast) and is regularly featured in leading publications including the Financial Times, BBC and Forbes.

- **Find out more:** work together, get in touch and join the mailing list: annaclareharper.com
- **Connect:** www.linkedin.com/annaclareharper
- **Access free articles:** annaclareharper.com/media-blog/
- **Listen to and subscribe to the podcast:** bit.ly/returnpodcast (search 'The Return: Property & Investment Podcast' on all other major platforms such as Spotify)
- **Get in touch:** hello@annaclareharper.com

YOU CAN ALSO CONNECT VIA:

@annaclareharper

@anna.clare.harper

@annaclareharperproperty

Printed in Great Britain
by Amazon

77496119R00139